What *Basketball FundaMENTALs* can do for you and your team . . .

"*Basketball FundaMENTALs* is an excellent book for the coach who wants to keep ahead of the game. With the game of basketball becoming more and more a game of the mind, this book offers the coach who practices its fundamentals a big edge over those who do not."
 —*Denny Crum, Head Basketball Coach, University of Louisville, 1980 and 1986 NCAA Champions*

"*Basketball FundaMENTALs* is the most complete book on fundamentals that I have ever read. It is a great teaching and learning tool for both coach and player."
 —*Lenny Wilkens, General Manager, Seattle Supersonics*

"This is a fantastic basketball training book. It should be in every young player's hands."
 —*Dale Brown, Head Basketball Coach, Louisiana State University*

"*Basketball FundaMENTALs* contains the easiest explanations for some of the most complex problems that must be met before excelling in the sport. The chapter on pressure is worth its weight in gold and is a must for anyone seeking the top levels of basketball."
 —*Johnny "Red" Kerr, former NBA star, coach, and general manager*

"A great book for coach and player both. It is very helpful in developing fundamentals and winning attitudes."
 —*Larry Brown, Head Basketball Coach, University of Kansas*

"*Basketball FundaMENTALs* is an excellent resource for teaching the all-important mental fundamentals of the game and is required reading for my team and staff. No coach or player should be without it."
 —*Willie Little, Head Basketball Coach, University of Illinois at Chicago*

"Excellent reading for young players who say they want to be great."
 —*Dr. Tom Davis, Head Basketball Coach, University of Iowa*

Basketball FundaMENTALs

A Complete Mental Training Guide

Jay Mikes

Leisure Press
Champaign, Illinois

Library of Congress Cataloging-in-Publication Data

Mikes, Jay, 1953-
    Basketball fundamentals.

    Bibliography: p.
    1. Basketball—Psychological
aspects.   2. Basketball—
Coaching.   I. Title.
GV889.2.M55   1987   796.32'3   86-19133
ISBN 0-88011-281-6

Developmental Editor: Linda Anne Bump
Copy Editor: Laura Larson
Assistant Editor: Sharon Kraus
Production Director: Ernie Noa
Assistant Production Director: Lezli Harris
Typesetter: Sandra Meier
Text Design: Julie Szamocki
Text Layout: Sandra Suzanne Lashmet
Illustrations by: Dan Halenza
Cover Photography: Focus West © 1986
Cover Design: Jack W. Davis
Printed by: Braun-Brumfield, Inc.

ISBN: 0-88011-281-6
Copyright © 1987 by Jay Mikes

Printed in the United States of America

10 9 8 7 6 5 4 3 2 1

Published by Leisure Press
A Division of Human Kinetics Publishers, Inc.
Box 5076, Champaign, IL 61820

To my wife, Kathy,
who demands teamwork,
pursues excellence,
and who keeps my vision of life
soft centered on the entire court.

Game Plan

Third Quarter: **Mental** *Practice*

Fourth Quarter: Game Fundamentals

Overtime

Showers

Foreword
by "The Coach"
Ray Meyer

For athletes to perform at the ultimate peak of their talents, they must be prepared mentally, emotionally, and physically. We, as coaches, have long understood the importance of this triad of preparation. Physical talent alone is not the total answer to winning. It is what you do with the talent that is important. And so we have attempted, each in our own way, to train our players in all areas of competition.

However, although our traditional coaching methods and practices have been long on the physical aspects of the game, they have been short on the mental and emotional elements of basketball. There are scores of excellent books and clinics available on the basic techniques and strategies of basketball. But there have been few books, if any, that have treated the mental, moral, and emotional elements of the game in an adequate way—until now.

The 1960s and 1970s revolutionized athletics by popularizing sophisticated strength training programs under the direction of professional instructors. In the last decade, we have witnessed another advance—a mental revolution in sports. We not only have numerous books available on sport psychology, but many major universities and professional franchises in all areas of sport have hired professional sport psychologists to train their athletes in a sophisticated way.

Although it is quite probable that your school or team does not have a full-time sport psychologist on hand, there is help available. *Basketball Fundamentals* provides an excellent opportunity for players and coaches to discover ways to gain an extra edge over their opponents. It is a vital tool in the preparation of the total athlete.

Preface

Sport psychology is a relatively new sport science, slipping its way into the consciousness of athletes and coaches alike. Much of the popular literature on the subject, however, is very general and is not easily applied by these readers. Perhaps this approach is why you and your coaches have not flocked to this promising new science. Nevertheless, basketball is undeniably ripe for the recent "discoveries" in sport psychology.

This book is intended as a practical, instructional guide for players and coaches. I hope that you will work through the information provided in this text under your coach's supervision. Accordingly, review questions are provided at the end of each chapter to promote discussion. By combining discussion and application, you can acquire a deeper understanding of the psychological concepts and techniques to which you have been introduced. However, you can also profit from *Basketball Fundamentals* without the help of your coach. I sincerely hope that every player and coach is able to discover a whole new approach to the quest for mastery of this great game!

Acknowledgments

First, I would like to thank Ron Cregier, Willie Little, Barb Zenner, Terry London, and Stan Kellner for their valuable comments that quite often sent me back to the drawing board for endless revision.

Second, I would like to thank Penny Hart for her efforts in coordinating the artwork. At the same time I would like to give special thanks to Darren Kairis for his help in preparing preliminary sketches. Finally, I am greatly indebted to Dan Halenza for his masterful illustrations.

Last but not least, I would like to thank my *Basketball Fundamentals* guinea pigs, the Bloomingdale Celtics, who assisted me in proving the value of the drills on the trampoline and balance beam. Thanks to "Jo Jo" Mikes, Mike "Fly" Watkins, Scott "The Colonel" Carnell, Mark "Alvan" Adamson, Freddie "Do-It-All" McFall, and Ivan "The Great" Daniels. Thanks also to James and Lucille Mikes for the use of their athletic facilities.

First Quarter: Mental Fundamentals

chapter 1

The Mental Revolution

Scan the books and magazine articles that are emerging on today's sports scene and you'll find a new focus for training athletes . . . an internal focus. The mental revolution in sports has arrived. Interestingly, these books and articles are not written by coaches but by experts in other fields. Impressive evidence has been gathered by psychologists, psychiatrists, kinesiologists, physiologists, physicians, and even theologians. They have removed many of the mysteries that once surrounded the "mental stuff" of athletic training. . . . The dramatic conclusion is that the power of the mind is the driving force behind all athletic achievement.
—Stan Kellner (1978, p. 96)

What separates the winner from the loser? Why does one athlete excel whereas another performs far below his or her potential? These are not easy questions. Yet they are at the crux of athletic competition. For years athletes, coaches, and fans have sought answers from the empirical evidence. They have pointed out the physical differences among athletes—size, speed, strength, and endurance. They have also pointed to the skill factor and the importance of mechanics and technique. When these components did not adequately explain the difference between "winners" and "losers," they pointed to the *mental* variables. Despite all the attention given to attitude, emotions, motivation, being "psyched up," and other vague explanations of mental preparedness, until quite recently there has never been an adequate explanation of the psychological factors of success. Although athletes have been given the right technique, the right exercises, the right meals, and the right equipment, they have rarely if ever received the right "psych job." As a result, many promising athletes have performed with mediocrity. How can all athletes come closer to realizing their potential? In other words, how can athletes, specifically basketball players, develop the *mental* fundamentals for outstanding performance? That is what this book is about. But before we reach the solution, we must fully understand the problem. The following short story begins to illustrate the problem of the underachieving athlete.

A Tale of Two Players

The bleachers were packed as John Walsh led the Lockport Lancers onto the court amid the deafening roar of the Lancer fans. It was state tournament time, and the Lancers had made it to the sectional finals against the third-rated team in the state, the Burlington Broncos. As John dribbled the ball at the head of the team in the Lancers' traditional warm-up lap around the court, his heart was pounding heavily, his breathing was shallow and rapid, and his muscles were tense. And why not? This was by far the biggest game of the year for the Lancers, who until the state tournament had experienced only moderate success. Now, if only they could manage one more victory, they would make the "big time."

Winning the sectional finals would mean a lot of recognition for the team because there were reporters present from the Chicago newspapers. But this game was also John's big chance to impress the college scouts who were at the game to see Ron Adamson, the Bronco's all-state candidate. John was secretly hoping to steal the limelight from the Bronco star. So, more than anything, he wanted this to be the best game of his high school career. He wanted the recognition for his team, but even more he wanted to impress the college scouts. On top of it all, the whole town of Lockport seemed to be at the game to cheer the team to victory. As the team's captain, John knew the fans were counting on him to lead the Lancers to their first appearance in the "Elite Eight." All these thoughts raced through John's mind as the Lancers were completing the warm-up lap and breaking into two lines for lay-ups.

John drove in, hit his first lay-up, and hustled back to the rebounding line. While waiting his turn to rebound,

John anxiously scanned the stands for his parents and new girlfriend, Laurie. He spotted them sitting ten rows up near center court. Laurie waved excitedly to John, who, of course, could not hear her cheers because of the deafening noise made by the school band. Nonetheless, he understood the message. He only hoped he and the team could come through with a miraculous win. "I *must* do it all and win tonight!" John thought as he ran in for the rebound and leaped high to tip in the missed lay-up.

When John returned to the shooting line, he felt an uneasiness in his stomach and his muscles were tied up in knots. He tried to tell himself to relax. But the more he tried to relax, the more uneasy he felt. He decided to ignore the tension for the moment, hoping it would go away once the game started.

After the Lancers went through 10 minutes of lay-ups, weaves, and other ball-handling drills, the squad split into two groups that took turns shooting outside shots. As John's partner was taking his turn shooting jump shots, John stood at half court and again glanced toward the stands to see where the college scouts were. He spotted them grouped together on the top row of the bleachers. Unfortunately, they were looking down at the other end of the gym, undoubtedly closely observing the opposing star, Ron Adamson. This made John even more determined to show the scouts what he could do.

When John's partner tossed him the ball, John immediately dribbled out to the wing to a spot over 20 feet from the basket. "After I hit a couple of 20-footers they'll be looking my way," he thought. But his first shots fell short, just barely hitting the front iron. On each missed attempt, he glanced to the stands to see if the scouts were looking his way. Fortunately, as he suspected, they were still watching Ron Adamson. John felt relieved but frustrated. He was relieved the scouts did not see his poor shooting, but he was angry they paid little attention to him. "I'll show them!" John thought. Gritting his teeth, he continued to cast 20-foot bombs at the basket. But as before, very few of his shots went in. The more he missed, the more frustrated he became. He knew he wasn't relaxing and following through, and he knew his shots had very little arc. "Oh, man! Is this going to be a bad night! I can't hit a thing!" he said to his shooting partner as he gave him the ball. "I just can't be off tonight! I can't!" Shaking his head, he stood at center court and watched the Burlington players warm up.

By this time the Burlington team was also performing its outside shooting drill. John saw Ron Adamson over by the sidelines awaiting his turn to shoot. Ron looked like he was off in his own world, constantly stretching out, tensing his muscles, and releasing the tension by shaking his arms and hands. Every once in a while Ron took a couple of deep breaths, shook his arms and hands, and let them hang limp. Then as if he were in a daze, Ron stared at the basket, oblivious to everything around him.

"What's with this guy?" John kept asking himself. "He looks like he couldn't care less about the game!"

John received the ball from his partner and once again went directly to the 20-foot range. As before, his shots went wide, fell short, and did everything but go in the basket. "Come on, you idiot! Put the ball in the hole!" he said under his breath. But as hard as he tried, John's usual arc and follow-through were missing. The downward spiral had begun. He was experiencing emotions he never knew existed. His tension and frustration continued to grow with each missed attempt, and his rhythm and confidence weakened. "I just can't be off tonight!"

At the other end of the gym, Ron Adamson had begun shooting his practice shots. But unlike John, Ron started by taking short, 10-foot jump shots inside the lane. This surprised John because Adamson was known as an excellent long-range shooter. Despite his reputation, Ron went up again and again for simple 10- and 12-foot jump shots inside the lane. As John watched Ron follow through on his shooting motion with grace and ease and hitting shot after shot, he asked himself why someone as good as Ron would take such simple shots. After all, more difficult shots would impress the scouts and fans. Surely he didn't expect such easy shots against Lockport—or did he? "I'll stop him," John assured himself.

Whereas John persistently shot from the outer limits, Ron continued his simple pregame ritual of stretching out, tensing his muscles, shaking them loose, breathing deeply, and focusing his attention on the basket. Only at the end of the warm-up session did Ron finally move away from the basket to take a few 15- to 20-foot jumpers. By then Ron was very loose and his shot dropped regularly. He felt ready; he was "psyched in."

As the buzzer sounded at the end of the warm-up period, both teams jogged to their respective benches to await the introductions of the starting line-ups. Both squads were very excited and enthusiastic. Several players yelled encouragement to their teammates; others were clapping and slapping "high fives." John felt intense and keyed up as he awaited his introduction to the fans. When his name was announced, he raced out onto the court to join the Lancers who had already been introduced. Again John's heart was pounding heavily and his palms were wet with perspiration as he greeted his teammates at center court. The Lockport fans let out a deafening roar. As the Lancer starting five returned to the bench, John raised a clenched fist to the fans, signaling that he was ready and confident. But John knew deep inside that he was not in control. He was tense and uncertain and secretly hoped luck would intervene and help him sink his first few shots. Once he began playing he would be alright.

As John stood with his team in front of the bench while the Burlington players were introduced, he kept a watchful eye on his Burlington counterpart, Ron Adamson. Unlike his teammates, Ron seemed aloof. He was very quiet, calm, and yet very absorbed. If he was concerned about the game's outcome and the presence of the scouts, he surely didn't show it. When introduced, Ron walked onto the court with purpose in his step and fire in his eyes.

The game began and Lockport controlled the opening tip. The Lancers played their patient "passing game" offense until John was free for a 16-foot jumper left of the key. He eyed the rim and shot with a perfect follow-through. John thought the shot felt good when the ball left his hands, but unfortunately, the ball went in and out. Burlington grabbed the rebound. As he raced downcourt to play defense, John complained inwardly, "Man, give me a break!"

At the other end of the court, Ron received the ball at the right wing and John closely guarded him. Ron pivoted back and forth and exploded toward the baseline where he pulled up for the short jumper. Ron had evaded John for just a moment, but John recovered quickly enough to contest the shot. As the ball soared through the air, the referee's whistle blew to stop the action. John watched the shot go through the net and then quickly looked at the referee. "Foul? I never touched him, Ref!" John screamed. The official gave John an annoyed look and warned, "Another outburst like that and you've got yourself a technical!" John had no alternative but to watch Ron hit the free throw to give Burlington a 3-0 lead.

John brought the ball upcourt, determined to make up for the last play. He neglected the team's offense, dribbled to the top of the key, and met a Bronco one-on-one for the jumper. But John's defensive man was tough and guarded him closely. In his determination and anxiety, John fired up a poor, off-balance shot. The ball barely grazed the rim and John knew right away he had compounded his problem.

As the game continued, John began to press more and more. With each missed shot his physical tension increased until he lost all rhythm and confidence. The basket, which on some nights had seemed as big as a rain barrel, now seemed as tiny as a teacup. He was shooting with no follow-through or backspin. His dribbling was hesitant, and his hands were unsure. He had become so tense and negative that he threw up an "air ball." In complete frustration, John followed the ball too aggressively and committed a silly foul that worsened his original mistake. His coach compassionately sat him on the bench—a loser.

John sat silently through the rest of the game and when he reflected on the evening, he could not help but admire Ron's performance. Ron did everything that night—scored, rebounded, hit the open player, and played defense. He had made some mistakes and missed some shots, too, but those plays did not seem to affect him. Perhaps it was his attitude that impressed John the most. Ron had that "something extra," something that John himself was missing. Now John could only sit and watch the seconds tick off the clock, as his high school career ended.

John, like many prep players, played very well in high school. Yet he knew he never realized his full potential, even though he had put in long hours perfecting his moves and jump shot and working hard with weights to develop his strength and quickness. He had done every drill imaginable. Why wasn't he the big star?

As John recalled his thoughts and emotions during the game and the ups and downs of his career, the answer became obvious. He had never met a player who had given him as much trouble as he had given himself.

The Moral

This story is, of course, fictional. Yet almost every high school basketball player experiences many of John's thoughts and feelings. Why do athletes feel such frustration?

The answer is simple. Coaches have almost entirely neglected the mental training of high school, college, and professional athletes. Although college and high school athletic programs have done much in the past few decades to train their athletes in the *physical* aspects of sports, they have done very little to train athletes in the *mental* aspects.

You might assume that athletes received little training in this area because coaches did not believe psychological factors were important. On the contrary, coaches have always believed the game's mental dimensions are very important ingredients of success. Consider all the times you have heard a coach say to a player, "Concentrate!" or "Relax!" But have you ever heard a coach explain *how* to relax and concentrate? Until recently very few coaches themselves knew enough about sport psychology to help their athletes.

Where to Begin

Today, sport is undergoing a mental revolution. In the last decade many books have been written about the mental side of sports. Relaxation, overcoming pressure, positive thinking, awareness and attention, mental and body rehearsal, and even the psychic/mystical side of sports have been discussed. Unfortunately, these books have been written either for sports in general or for sports other than basketball. When it comes to mental training specifically for basketball, hardly any resources exist. Stan Kellner has written an excellent book, *Taking It to the Limit*,[1] that I recommend to every player interested in improving his or her game. Stan's book tells how an athlete may improve through mental rehearsal. This book, *Basketball Fundamentals*, is intended to explore further the mental side of basketball.

Purpose of the Book

The principal purpose of *Basketball Fundamentals* is to introduce you to the *mental* fundamentals of basketball.

---

[1]For a copy of Stan's book, *Taking It to the Limit* (1978), write to Stan Kellner, P.O. Box 134, East Setauket, New York, 11733.

To do so, the book is designed to meet the following objectives:

1. **To develop your power of concentration on the court.** You will learn the proper focus of attention for each phase of the game—shooting, ball handling, defense, and rebounding. You will also learn to use your power of concentration in practice to develop your physical and mental skills.
2. **To teach you how to relax and maintain your composure on the court.** You will acquire new attitudes and habits that will help you overcome pressure, play at optimum intensity, and let your body and mind work in harmony.
3. **To help you to develop the essential quality of true confidence enabling you to become a clutch performer.** You will learn how to control your mind and body when the game is on the line.
4. **To put consistency into your game so you play well game after game.** Your newly developed mind control will enable you to avoid the ups and downs that typically mark a season. You will soon have fewer off nights.

The Tip-Off

To achieve these objectives, *Basketball Fundamentals* covers many topics, combining the expertise and wisdom of top coaches, star athletes, psychologists, and educators. Some of the ideas in this book are tainted by personal perspective, but many are simply a blend of knowledge from several sources and authorities. Much of my motivation to write this book was a desire to whittle down the growing knowledge of sport psychology to the size of a small handbook applied strictly to basketball. As a result, I attempted to balance comprehensiveness and economy, trying to say only enough to be clear without overdoing it. In reading the text, you will discover that many of the topics are closely related. Rather than restating points made in other sections of the text, I have referred to the related section for further study.

I recommend you read through this book at least twice: once to become familiar with the material and a second time to clarify and reinforce your understanding of new ideas.

Then keep the book on hand for easy reference when specific problems and questions arise.

Your introduction to the mental facets of the game begins with an explanation of "The Three Cs of Peak Performance." In this chapter you will explore the meaning of concentration, confidence, and composure and discover how these qualities are essential to athletic performance.

The chapters "Skill and Body Awareness" and "Developing the Master Sense" are perhaps the two key chapters of the book. The first introduces you to your sense of body awareness and tells you how to improve it and use it on the court. Most importantly, this chapter explains why body awareness is crucial to developing basketball skills. The next chapter introduces you to the master sense—mind awareness. You will discover the importance of flexible attention on the court. You will also learn how to use mind awareness to develop mind control and concentration. And you will receive practical advice on how to use mind awareness on the court during practice and games.

The game plan for the second quarter, Fundamental Skills, is to give you an in-depth explanation of the specific concentration you should have for each phase of the game. The chapters "Shooting Fundamentals," "Shooting Slumps," "Free Throw Fundamentals," "Ball-Handling Fundamentals," "Defensive Fundamentals," and "Rebounding Fundamentals" focus on psychological elements of each skill.

Chapter 11, "Intensity," gives you an insight into the optimum intensity levels for offense, defense, and rebounding. It also contrasts the moral and emotional bases of intensity.

The importance of "Quickness" and the factors contributing to it are discussed next. Chapter 12 shows how quickness is largely mental in nature and how proper awareness, instant reaction, and anticipation are all essential elements of quickness.

At Halftime we will take a break from the basketball action for an interesting interview on the mental fundamentals of weight training. In "The Mind in Athletics and Strength Training," we will look at the mental aspects of what is now an integral part of a basketball player's training program. This section also describes the importance of the subconscious mind in athletic training and shows why an athlete must set clear goals.

The strategy for the third quarter, Mental Practice, is to develop your mental skills and show you how to use two types of mental practice methods. "Suggestology and Mental Rehearsal: Easy Chair Drills" describes mental drills and activities you can do while sitting down or laying in bed. "Mind Games" describes drills that promote awareness, concentration, balance, and motor coordination.

In the fourth quarter we will change strategies and look at Game Fundamentals. Chapter 16, "Pressure and the Emotional Elements of Sports," describes the emotions that affect an athlete's performance. It then explains the nature of pressure, looks at its sources, and prescribes ways to deal with it. In "Pregame Programming and Postgame Analysis," you will learn what to do to prepare for a game and for the critical first 2 minutes of each half. You will discover the importance of being mentally active, not emotionally high.

Because momentum is such an important key to victory, a short chapter is devoted to that topic. In "Momentum," you will find out how your frame of mind (positive or negative) can shift momentum in your favor.

To bring out the clutch performer in you, "When the Game Is on the Line" (chapter 20) describes the intricate web of mind awareness, good habits, concentration, control, confidence, composure, and clutch performance.

In Overtime, we will depart from the psychological aspects and delve into other mental facets of the game. In "Basketballology 101" and "Most Valuable Player," the emphasis is on basketball knowledge rather than psychology. In the first of these chapters you will learn the importance of being a student of the game. In the second you will be given standards to follow as a player and criteria to judge the quality of other players. Sandwiched between these two chapters is a chapter on "The Moral Elements" of basketball that addresses the personal qualities of selflessness, leadership, sportsmanship, respect for authority, and commitment to excellence.

The concluding chapter is a final word on the mental aspects of basketball. I hope this final message will inspire you to pursue your "Inner Horizons."

Although this book does not detail each and every thought on the mental aspects of basketball, it will serve players and coaches alike as a valuable guide to the long overlooked mental fundamentals. It offers no miracles, just straightforward information and practical advice on how to use our growing knowledge of psychology in athletics. No matter what level of competition you're associated with— high school, college, or pro—there is something in this book for you. *Basketball Fundamentals* may not make you an all-star, but it will make you a better player. It does not guarantee that you will be a champion, but it will enable you to overcome your toughest opponent—you.

Questions for Review

1. What pressures did John feel during warm-ups?
2. What physical sensations did John experience because of these feelings? Have you ever experienced similar sensations and feelings?
3. Compare the type of shots John took during warm-ups against those Ron took during warm-ups. Which is a better way to warm up? Why?
4. How did John react when he missed shots during warm-ups?
5. Describe Ron's warm-up routine. What purpose did it serve?
6. Describe John's emotional and physical feelings during the game. How did they affect his performance?
7. Explain what the last sentence means: "He had never met a player who had given him as much trouble as he had given himself."

chapter 2

The Three Cs of Peak Performance

With or without—but hopefully with—a coach's help, the athlete of today must learn to gain control over both physiological and psychological processes. . . . The key to all this is to learn to relax and then to learn how and where to direct attentional processes. . . . A relaxed athlete is a confident athlete, and the sooner individuals comprehend this, the better they will perform.
—Robert Nideffer (1976, pp. 89, 106)

Take a moment to recall the best game you ever played. Relive the sights, sounds, and body sensations of that day. Do this by closing your eyes and picturing the court, your opponent, your teammates, the fans, and the action. Can you remember the spectacular plays? Let your imagination run for several replays until you recreate vivid images of the sensations you experienced. What were they like? Don't jump ahead to the next paragraph until you have actually relived those special moments.

Besides very vivid sensory experiences, you more than likely had some positive feelings during the game. Take a moment now to recall the feelings you had that day. Were you relaxed or tense? Assertive or passive? Confident or worried? Did you lose your temper, become frustrated, or sulk? Or were you generally composed and in control?

If you are like most athletes, during your peak performance you experienced quite vividly the three essential ingredients of athletic success: concentration, composure, and confidence. Blended together, these ingredients conspired to raise your consciousness to a high plateau and to reveal a dimension of athletics you never knew existed.

Although the effects of the Three Cs on athletic achievement are legendary, they are not always readily available or easy to find. For some athletes they are forever elusive. For others they are fleeting. But for the chosen few, the peak performers, they are always on hand.

In this chapter we will examine the Three Cs of peak performance—concentration, composure, and confidence—and look at their effect on athletic performance. In the end you will know what it is like to think like a winner. Then in the remainder of the book, you will learn proven methods to help you develop your court concentration, composure, and confidence.

The First Ingredient: Concentration

In *Peak Performance*, Charles Garfield (1984) identifies eight physical and mental conditions that elite athletes describe as characterizing the feelings they have at those moments when they are performing extraordinarily well. Of these eight peak performance feelings, three are associated with high levels of concentration. First, athletes are *mentally relaxed*. They feel an "inner calm" and "a sense of time being slowed down." The underachiever, on the other hand, experiences a lot of mental tension. He or she suffers from a loss of concentration and a sense of things "happening too fast" and feeling "out of control."

The second feeling of peak performance is a sense of being *focused on the present*. Athletes report a feeling of "harmony between mental and physical," between mind and body. They are absorbed in the present with no thoughts or feelings about the past or future.

Third, athletes are in a state of *extraordinary awareness*. They are "acutely aware of their bodies and of the athletes around them." They experience heightened powers of anticipation and response. All their actions are automatic and effortless (Garfield, 1984, pp. 158-159).

What is similar about the feelings "being focused on the present," "a sense of time being slowed down," "extraordinary awareness," and being "acutely aware of their bodies and of the athletes around them"? They all have to do with *sensory awareness*. The type of concentration a player has when he or she is "on" involves thoughts that are pure sensory awareness, specifically visual awareness.

The uninterrupted concentration on pure sensory awareness, particularly visual awareness, creates the illusion of "time slowed down." In this state of awareness, the athlete sees objects and events more clearly and seems to have more time to make the right decisions. On the other hand, when an athlete's visual awareness is interrupted by imagination (fears, anxieties, or frustrations); by verbal, self-critical thoughts ("You clutz! Catch the ball!"); by verbal aggression ("Gee whiz, Ref!"); or by sensory awareness (muscle tension, fatigue, or pain); then the athlete's visual awareness suffers and "everything happens too fast."

Mental Movies

The difference between uninterrupted and interrupted visual awareness can be seen in the following example. Imagine you are watching a short film of three teammates being guarded man-to-man. In this film one teammate breaks free of a defender and gets open for a pass. Your task is to spot the open player immediately and call out his or her name while dribbling a basketball. Normally this is not very difficult. But the film is only 25 frames long and has been edited.

The Underachiever's Mental Movie. For the classic under-achiever the mental movie might appear in the following sequence. When the movie begins, Frames 1 through 3 give you a quick glimpse of the initial setup. However, during Frames 4 through 9 you hear a voice shouting at you, causing you to shift your attention to the sound. You instinctively return your attention to the film and can see Frames 10 through 13. These frames show the receivers faking one way and beginning to move the other direction. Unfortunately, when Frames 14 through 19 flash on the screen, you see a close-up of the defender guarding you. The film then cuts back to action for Frames 20 through 23 where it appears one player is about to get a step on his or her defender and break free. But before you can get a good look to assess the situation, you misdribble the ball and must look at it to recover it. When you refocus your vision on the screen, all you see are the words *Too late!* printed in white on a black background.

All this happens, of course, in just a few seconds. In those few seconds you have only three fraction-of-a-second glimpses to locate the open player and to react. In the situation described the distractions have reduced the vital information to only 11 frames as opposed to the original 25. In effect, the vital information "happens too fast."

The Peak Performer's Mental Movie. After a few frustrating moments you are shown a second version of the film, only this time the film is unedited and there are no distractions. You now can view 25 uninterrupted frames of the three players cutting to get open. In this second situation, the film of uninterrupted vital information is more than twice as long, creating an effect of "time slowing down."

The two movies vividly depict the difference between the concentration of the peak performer and the under-achiever. The underachiever lets unnecessary disruptions enter the stream of consciousness whereas the peak per-former is able to maintain visual concentration. By increasing the amount of vital data being fed into his or her mind, the star player increases the chances of selecting the right response in a given situation and of having a better "physi-cal" performance. In brief, the star player's output (perfor-mance) is greater because the input (concentration) is superior.

Centering

A key concept in understanding concentration is the mental process of *centering*. Centering is the mental process of tuning in to one thought channel while tuning out the other channels. In a sense, your mind is like a television set. There are several channels to pick, and although you can switch from channel to channel, you cannot put more than one image on the screen at a time. Figure 2.1 illustrates the various channels on which your mind can center.

When you center on your visual system, you are more aware of visual objects but are less aware of messages from your senses of hearing, touch, and balance; your body awareness; verbal thoughts; and other information channels. Also, if you focus on one of these senses (sensations exist in the *present*), you cannot also watch "replays" of *past* sensory images. Likewise, if your mind is switched to your imagination, recalling past sense experiences, you cannot focus on present sensations or on your "inner voice." You're lucky this is true; imagine what it would be like to have all of your mental TV channels showing on your screen at once. It would be totally confusing!

Your mind is selective in what it focuses on; you cannot be centering on two or more channels at the same time. But you can alternate your centering between channels. As one channel holds your attention, the others tend to fade into the background of your mind.

To illustrate the importance of proper centering, imagine yourself receiving the short inbounds pass against a full-court zone press. At this moment two defenders converge

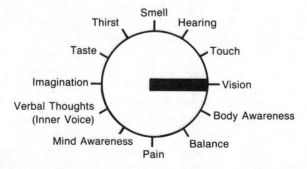

Figure 2.1   Mental channels.

on you for the double-team. What do you think will happen if, rather than centering on your visual system looking for open receivers, your mind briefly recalls the turnover you made the last time you were clamped in a double-team? On the other hand, think how easy it is to spot an open player if your mind is not distracted. When two defensive players are trying to double-team you, at least one offensive player is left unguarded. Hitting the open player is essentially a problem of seeing the opening, not a problem of passing technique. As a result, if you have proper visual concentration, breaking the press is very easy to do. But if you have poor visual awareness, breaking the press becomes very difficult. In short, breaking the press is more mental than physical.

Soft Centering Versus Fine Centering

Although the previous example illustrates the importance of proper centering, in basketball there is more to court concentration than tuning in to the right channel. In some situations on the court you need very specific information. In other situations you need to see the larger picture. The difference in the type of information needed is illustrated by the difference between shooting, on one hand, and playing defense when your player does not have the ball on the other. When shooting you should focus specifically on the basket, which is a very narrow focus of attention. When playing defense off the ball, you must see your player and the player with the ball. In this case, your field of vision may need to include the entire court.

The terms we will use throughout the remainder of this book to differentiate between a broad and narrow focus of attention will be the terms suggested by Weiskopf (1975), *soft centering* and *fine centering*. Soft centering refers to a *broad* focus of attention within a sensory system. It means focusing on the entire court and being aware of everything within your field of vision. Fine centering refers to a *narrow* focus of attention within a sensory system. An example of fine centering is focusing specifically on the basket when shooting. Knowing the difference between these two types of centering is crucial to understanding the remainder of the book. Their meaning will become clear as we explore the fundamental skills in the next section.

Wrap-Up

In order to perform at your best you must learn to control your concentration. You must develop habits of expanding or contracting the scope of your vision to the proper degree of softness or fineness depending on the situation and task at hand. The proper concentration for each phase of the game—shooting, ball handling, rebounding, and defense—is discussed in the next section, Second Quarter: Fundamental Skills, in which one chapter is devoted to each fundamental.

The Second Ingredient: Composure

The closely interwoven relationship between concentration and the second ingredient of peak performance, composure, is clearly described in *The Inner Athlete*. Nideffer (1976) explains that practitioners of the martial arts are trained to remain calm and composed under highly stressful situations. Martial art students learn to make their minds "like still water." On a calm day the surface of a pond is smooth, creating a natural mirror. When the water is disturbed by a tossed pebble, for example, the reflections in the water become broken and distorted. Martial arts experts believe that emotions (fear, anger, anxiety, frustration, or depression) do to the mind what a pebble or the wind does to the surface of a pond; that is, emotions distort perception and make it nearly impossible to react appropriately.

Composure, or controlling one's emotions, was cited in two of Garfield's eight peak performance feelings. Not surprisingly, the primary feeling of being "mentally relaxed," cited in the discussion of concentration, also applies to composure. Garfield (1984) explains the additional concept of being in a "cocoon" of concentration. This feeling, often experienced by peak performers, is a sense of being insulated from the anxiety or fear ordinarily associated with challenging athletic situations. Within the cocoon, the athlete can avoid a loss of concentration; the sense of everything happening too fast; and the tense, out-of-control feelings brought about by overarousal. In short, concentration depends on composure. An athlete cannot perceive a situation accurately without first controlling his or her emotions.

The Underachiever's Negative Feelings

Although discussing the feelings of peak performance helps us to understand how emotions affect athletic performance, considering the negative feelings of fear, anxiety, frustration, anger, and depression experienced by the underachiever may be even more enlightening. In examining the negative emotions, we will first look at the physiological aspect of these feelings, the well-known "fight-or-flight" syndrome.

Fight-or-Flight. The changes your body undergoes when you are confronted with a threatening or stressful situation are known as the fight-or-flight syndrome. This syndrome is an inborn, physiological response mechanism that literally prepares your body for fighting or fleeing in the face of danger. The mechanics of fight-or-flight are simple. When you are faced with a threatening or stressful situation, your brain sends a signal to your pituitary gland that in turn stimulates the adrenal glands to secrete hormones. These hormones rush through your body and prepare your muscles for action. Your muscles tense, your heartbeat and breathing speed up, your blood flows from your skin and extremities to your large muscles, and your digestive system shuts down. As a result, your muscles quiver, your heart pounds, your lungs pant, and you look pale and feel nauseous. These bodily reactions are mentally distracting because they are so abnormal. You are forced to focus on them instead of on your task, and as a result your visual field becomes very narrow. In almost every case the overaroused athlete suffers from tunnel vision.

How do these physiological reactions affect performance? Thomas Tutko and Umberto Tosi, coauthors of *Sports Psyching* (1976), explain that sometimes the fight-or-flight response can be beneficial. Quick bursts of energy provided by the response may fuel supernormal performances. Unfortunately, the anxieties causing the fight-or-flight response will more likely distort perception of the situation and disrupt performance. This reminds us again of the martial arts experts who suggest that fear does to the mind what a pebble does to the surface of a pond; that is, it distorts perceptions and ruins judgment. Moreover, highly charged emotions affect the athlete's body by creating higher than normal muscle tension, which in turn disrupts coordination, timing, and composure.

Fear, Anxiety, Anger, and Frustration. The emotions that most commonly trigger the fight-or-flight syndrome and prevent an athlete from playing up to his or her potential are fear, anxiety, anger, and frustration. Fear and anger are the most disruptive emotions because the objects of these emotions are generally clear and present. Fear is the strong urge to flee in the face of an immediate danger, such as the sound of a gunshot or the pressure of being double-teamed in basketball. Anxiety, on the other hand, is accompanied by a mild urge to flee because the thing feared (generally a loss or a poor performance) exists in the future and not the immediate present. In both cases, anxiety and fear, the player responds to some degree with the symptoms of the fight-or-flight syndrome.

Depression. A player's performance can also be affected in quite a different way from the overarousal or overexcitement of the fight-or-flight syndrome. A player's performance frequently suffers from underarousal or lack of excitement caused by a depression rooted in feelings of apathy, indifference, and powerlessness. For an athlete, depression means sluggish movement and low energy levels. It is just the opposite of the highly energized state that the peak performer experiences. The effects of depression involve more than low energy; research (Durden-Smith & de Simone, 1983) has shown that it impairs skills as well.

So what does all this mean? It means that no matter why an athlete performs poorly—poor concentration, a lack of confidence, an inability to control anger and other emotions, limited physical attributes, or lack of skill—he or she may compound the problem by slipping into the emotional rut of depression. Unless this emotional state is corrected, poor performance becomes a habit. Depression affects the mental and physical habits of every phase of basketball—shooting, ball handling, rebounding, and defense. Thus the athlete may become caught in a downward spiral. Poor performance leads to apathy and depression; apathy and depression result in unspirited play; and unspirited play results in even worse performance.

The Peak Performer's Feelings

The peak performer's feelings are just the opposite of the underachiever's. Rather than feeling anxious, apathetic and depressed, the peak performer feels highly energized. In his discussion of the eight feelings of peak performance, Charles Garfield (1984) explains that the peak performer's intensity does not relate to the negative emotions of fear, anger, and anxiety but more to the positive feelings associated with high energy. *Joy, ecstasy,* and *power* are often used to describe the feelings.

The Joy of Success. Joy is the elation we experience when we have reached a goal and always comes with a reduction of the tensions that accompany the goal, such as the desire to win. When an individual reaches a goal—that is, when the athlete plays well or wins—tensions surrounding the goal are released. If a goal such as winning is not realized, or a release from tension does not occur, the individual does not feel joy. In fact, the unreleased tensions may lead to frustration (Silverman, 1971).

Look for a Challenge. This means that in order to derive pleasure and joy from athletics, you must pursue a goal that you think is not easy to reach. What's the excitement in defeating a weak opponent who had little chance of beating you? Destroying a weak team may inflate your ego, but it will not stir your emotions. The thrill of victory comes only when there is a good chance you won't experience it. To get the most out of athletics, you must look for a challenge, whether it be a tough schedule, the pursuit of excellence, or a performance goal other than winning. Admittedly, putting yourself on the line like that can create fear, anxiety, anger, frustration, and depression. But that's part of the great challenge of sports. You put yourself on an emotional high wire and see if you can maintain your emotional balance with concentration and confidence.

Healthy Sensitivity. An athlete should try to attain what Thomas Tutko and Umberto Tosi (1976) call *healthy sensitivity.* You must try to derive pleasure and satisfaction from successful plays and not become overly upset when you make mistakes. The goal is not for you to eliminate emotions from athletics by ignoring the emotional content of sports. You must seek the joy of success and learn to overcome your fears, anxieties, frustrations, anger, or depression.

The Third Ingredient:
Confidence

This game is all confidence, and, you know, sometimes it's
scary. When I'm at my best, I can do just about anything I
want, and no one can stop me. I feel like I'm in total
control of everything.
—Larry Bird (in Callahan, March 18, 1985, p. 53)

Coming from the greatest basketball player today, these thoughts are extremely enlightening, especially when you consider the basis of Bird's greatness. Most experts agree that Bird is relatively "unathletic" compared to some tremendous athletes in the NBA. He is not physically quick and cannot jump. He relies on sheer skill. Skill, unlike athletic ability, is heavily dependent on the mental aspects of the game—concentration, composure, and confidence.

By now, you may be beginning to realize that the Three Cs are completely interdependent. Each C has a profound effect on the other two. Confidence and a positive attitude result in less anxiety, less muscle tension, and greater concentration. Without confidence, the first two Cs would be like a three-legged stool missing the third leg. Without confidence the stool collapses; with confidence, it stands steady and firm.

Again referring to Garfield's work, two of the eight peak performance feelings relate somehow to confidence. Peak performers are "confident and optimistic, with a generally positive outlook" (1984, p. 159). They feel totally "in control" with no deliberate effort to *exert* control. "There is a definite sense of being able to make all the right moves." Notice how directly these feelings match Larry Bird's peak performance feelings.

Negative Thinking

Perhaps it is easiest to understand how confidence helps peak performance by looking at how negative feelings affect performance. A lack of self-confidence influences performance in two ways. First, negative thinking can become a self-fulfilling prophecy. Athletes who do not believe in their abilities put forth less effort. They hold back so that they can use lack of effort as an excuse for not being successful. In a sense, fear and anxiety over the possibility of failure keep some athletes from giving it their all. As the saying goes, "No guts, no glory!" The underachiever's reaction to the fear of failure actually prevents him or her from ever achieving success.

A second problem of negative thinking involves the fact that our thoughts direct our bodies. Any player who holds negative images about his or her ability to dribble cannot help but dribble poorly because the mental pictures show vague or uncoordinated movements. On the other hand, any player who holds positive, clear images about his or her dribbling skill is likely to be a good dribbler because those positive images direct the body. A lack of confidence is generally a result of negative self-images, whereas confidence is a result of positive self-images or believing in yourself.

Positive Thinking

Positive thinking is, by definition, positive. The positive thinker does not let his or her mind dwell on negative thoughts. However, positive thinking differs from wishful thinking. Positive thinking must have an element of reality or possibility to improve your performance effectively. Those positive thoughts that you do not honestly believe to be true are actually *wishful thinking*. Your mind only accepts and acts according to what it truly believes to be real. Telling yourself you are going to have a hot shooting night does not reduce your anxiety over an upcoming performance unless you have *true* confidence in your shooting skill.

For the most part, believing in yourself and your skills comes from experience. For example, if you have been successful in the past at some skill, such as shooting, you may be truly confident at performing that skill in the future. You are confident because you have clear mental images of performing that skill well in the past. On the other hand, if you have not developed your skill and you do not have prior successful experiences, you have no legitimate basis for having confidence in your shooting skill (no matter what else you tell yourself). This lack of *true* confidence threatens your composure and creates anxiety, and the anxiety of failure breaks your concentration and produces excessive muscle tension.

Confidence Under Game Conditions

Besides being confident in your skills, to be a consistent peak performer you must be confident of being confident. That is, you must be confident that you have the psychological skills to control the Three Cs during competition. If you cannot relax enough to reduce your physical and mental tension during games, all the wishful (but positive) thinking in the world will not enable you to relax and be confident in important games. Shooting well in practice is not enough. Every athlete knows that skill in practice and skill in pressure game situations are two very different things. This in itself may cause anxiety. If you're not in control of the Three Cs, you won't be in control of your basketball skills.

Developing Confidence

Confidence in any skill is largely a matter of learning, practice, and having had prior successful experience. Or in John Wooden's words, "Confidence comes from being prepared" (Wooden & Tobin, 1973, p. 91). If you want to develop total confidence in your game, you must totally prepare yourself for competition—physically, mentally, and emotionally. You must develop the proper techniques and concentration of shooting, ball handling, defense, and rebounding. Second, and just as important, you must develop relaxation skills and the proper attitudes that help you control your emotions and physical tension. Finally, you must get yourself in excellent physical condition through strength training and endurance training programs. If you dedicate yourself to total preparation, you will know that you are ready to play your best.

Summary

Playing up to your potential involves three essential ingredients—concentration, composure, and confidence. In order for you to play your best you must concentrate, keep your emotions under control, and believe in your ability. Again, by belief in your ability I mean more than just the belief in your basketball skills. You must believe in your psychological skills, that is, the ability to concentrate and to control your emotions during stressful game situations. It is not enough to have one or two of these ingredients because all three are so intricately interwoven. The more you have of one, the more you can develop the others. The less you have of one, the less likely you are to maintain the others. The rest of this book is designed to tell you exactly how to develop each of these qualities of peak performance.

Questions for Review

1. Name the Three Cs of peak performance.
2. Identify the feelings associated with good concentration.

3. Compare the concentration or "mental movie" of the underachiever with that of the peak performer.
4. What does the term "centering" mean?
5. What is the difference between fine centering and soft centering?
6. Why is composure (i.e., control of one's emotions) an essential ingredient of peak performance?
7. Identify some physical responses of the fight-or-flight syndrome.
8. How does the fight-or-flight syndrome affect athletic performance?
9. Identify five emotions that prevent an athlete from playing up to his or her potential.
10. Why is confidence or a positive attitude an essential ingredient of peak performance?
11. What is the difference between positive thinking and wishful thinking?
12. What is meant by "having confidence in your psychological skills"? Why is it important?

chapter 3

Skill and
Body Awareness

*In our culture relatively little importance has been
given to body awareness. The emphasis is on
achievement rather than on awareness. Yet it is only
those athletes who have a highly developed
kinesthetic sense—muscle sense—who ever achieve
high levels of excellence. One simply can't play any
sport well lacking the ability to focus carefully on the
subtle body sensations which indicate the difference
between balance and off-balance, timing and mis-
timing, too tight and too loose. Body awareness is
directly related to body achievement.*
—W. Timothy Gallwey (1976, p. 73)

Because the objective of the game is to put the ball in
the basket, skill in handling the ball is crucial. Either you
must shoot accurately from long distances, or you must advance the ball toward the basket for close-in shots. Advancing the ball requires passing, receiving, dribbling, and faking
skills.

Developing the proper technique and the fine coordination of basketball skills can be enhanced by a keen sense
of body awareness. Singer (1972) tells us that body awareness is an important part of the learning process. Many
athletes are encouraged to "feel the act" and be aware of
the changing positions of the body parts and their relation
to each other as they learn to perform a skill. However, when
these skills become highly developed and routine, an athlete
performs them without thinking about his or her body. Athletes who demonstrate outstanding skill in general seem to
have a keenly developed sense of body awareness. Top offensive performers like Michael Jordan, Mark Aguirre, and Isiah
Thomas can undoubtedly attribute their shooting and

"shake-and-bake" offensive moves to fine kinesthetic or muscle sense. For the beginner as well as the advanced performer, body awareness is the key to developing and refining skills.

Increasing Awareness

W. Timothy Gallwey (1976) says the skill-learning process can be summarized in two words—*increasing awareness*. Whether you are learning the fine skills of shooting and ball handling or the more basic skills of running and jumping, increasing your awareness is the key to learning. If you want to improve your basketball skills, you must first increase your body awareness.

Focusing on Body Awareness

Body awareness refers to the feelings or sensations of contracting and relaxing muscles and the movement of the body in space. When you feel sore, tense, or tired, you are experiencing body awareness. The important thing for you, the athlete, is that your sense of body awareness lets you know the position of your limbs from the feedback received from your muscles. As a result, you do not need to see yourself move to realize you're moving, and you do not need to see your limbs to know what position they are in. You can *feel* it.

Prove this to yourself with a simple exercise. Extend your right arm out to your side so it is parallel to the floor. Without looking at your arm, bend your arm at the elbow to a 90° angle. Now look at your arm. Is your arm bent at a 90° angle? Of course. How were you able to do this? Body awareness!

Now try something else. (You can put your arm down now.) While sitting in a chair, straighten your right leg by extending your lower leg in front of you. As soon as your leg is extended, point your toes. As you begin the exercise, center your attention on body awareness. Close your eyes and focus your attention on your thighs. Try to feel the contraction of your leg muscles as you lift your lower leg and increase the tension in your thighs. Which muscles do you feel contracting as you point your toes? Which muscles do you feel stretching?

Close your eyes again for a moment and do a quick survey of your body using your muscle sense. As you feel your muscles from the inside, is there any tension? Are your back, neck, or shoulders tense or relaxed? Can you feel the muscles that contract when you move your head to the right? Can you feel the muscles that stretch?

Imagine yourself at the free throw line, and go through your shooting motion. Does your arm extend out or up toward the basket? Is your elbow in? Does your wrist flex on your follow-through? Is your shooting arm tense or relaxed?

As you think about the exercises you just performed, you will realize that the more you were aware of your muscles through your muscle sense, the less you were aware of the sensations of your other sensory systems. Also, when you centered on your muscles you were focusing on the present. It is impossible to think in the past or in the future (using your imagination) if you are concentrating on one of your senses. This is important because when developing a skill in practice, you must maintain your concentration on your senses. You cannot let your mind wander. By maintaining your concentration on body awareness, you improve the feedback your mind receives that is the key to learning. But we will discuss that in a minute. For now, welcome to the world of your muscles, where you will dwell often if you are to become a highly skilled player.

Improving Body Awareness

If body awareness is critical in developing skill, it makes sense to try to improve your sense of body awareness. The problem is how to sharpen this sense.

A possible solution might be to practice activities where an increase (both in quantity and quality) in body awareness experiences is present. A different sport provides good examples of such activities.

Of all sports, gymnastics is perhaps the one that requires the greatest sense of body awareness and balance. The gymnast's focus of attention is almost entirely inward because of the intricate moves involved in each event. Because body awareness helps basketball players refine intricate skills in their sport, we basketball players can benefit from becoming part-time gymnasts much like we have become part-time weight lifters to become stronger. The gymnastic activities we should do most are those in which our senses of balance and body awareness are heightened beyond what we are used to as basketball players. Of course, the most helpful activities are those that are like our own game and that we can adapt to serve our purposes. There is not much point in developing specific gymnastic skills that have no relation to basketball.

The two gymnastics events that meet these criteria are the balance beam and the trampoline. Both events develop the senses of balance and body awareness to different degrees. In effect, they put the athlete in an environment or situation that heightens the awareness of these senses. Thus they give us a substantial amount of feedback for developing balance and coordination.

Gymnastic Activities Applied to Basketball. Although developing a general sense of balance and coordination is beneficial, developing these senses as they specifically apply to basketball is even more helpful. Performing flips on the trampoline or cartwheels on the balance beam is unnecessary. The best drills are those that emphasize simple vertical movement (simple bouncing and jumping) and pivoting or twisting movement (180° to 360° turns). Later, after you have developed some general balance and coordination skills and have become more confident, the tasks on the equipment will involve ball-handling skills that focus on developing visual control along with body awareness.

I derived the idea for using this type of drill from Weiskopf (1975) and from the experiences of William Natale, a personal friend who benefitted from similar drills as a minor league baseball player at the Kansas City Royals Baseball Academy in Sarasota, Florida. I believe the trampoline and balance beam drills are better adapted to basketball than baseball (see chapter 4, "Developing the Master Sense" and chapter 15, "Mind Games").

Safety Considerations. *Safety* should always be an important consideration in any practice situation, but in the trampoline and balance beam drills it becomes an even greater concern because of your possible lack of skill and the very nature of the gymnastics equipment. The trampoline drills should be done *only* on a trampoline that either is built into the ground so the bed is ground level or has a platform built around it so the bed is level with the platform when spotters are present. These precautions not only make the drills safer, but they also reduce the athlete's anxiety. Many states have outlawed the use of trampolines in schools. Before implementing a trampoline training program, the coach must find out the legal status of the trampoline in your state.

The balance beam, which is safer than the trampoline, can easily be built by nailing together a few pieces of two-by-four. When constructed as shown in Figure 3.1, the athlete performing the balance beam drills is no more than 6 inches off the floor. If the athlete loses his or her balance, which is common, he or she can simply step off.

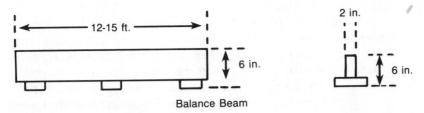

Balance Beam

Figure 3.1 Balance beam for body awareness drills.

Increasing Basketball Skills Through Body Awareness

Shooting skill is developed through a learning process in which the mind subconsciously weaves an intricately patterned response of muscle contraction and relaxation (coordination). When you shoot, your mind sends out electrical impulses to specific sets of muscles, causing some to contract and others to relax. Although you do not know specifically how many and which particular muscle fibers are contracting, you do have general impressions of which muscles are working and which are not through your sense of body awareness.

Feedback from your muscles and the visual feedback of the result (hit or miss) let you know whether your mind's directions to your muscles were accurate. Your skill develops as you learn which directions are accurate and which are not in a process of trial and error involving repetition after repetition. In general, the more experiences you have, the more able you are to distinguish good and bad directions and responses.

As your mind collects its data, it begins to organize the information for future reference. Each experience leaves an impression on the subconscious mind, creating a "muscle memory," and this muscle memory is recalled each time a similar experience occurs. Actions, then, are based on past experiences or muscle memory. For example, when you are about to shoot a free throw, your mind recalls the proper coordination for shooting a free throw based on the thousands of your past experiences shooting free throws. This process happens every time you perform any basketball skill.

In other words, learning occurs and skill develops according to two principles. First, the more experiences you have, the greater the imprint is on your mind. Second, the clearer the feedback is, the stronger the imprint is on your mind. And the stronger the imprint is on your mind, the more developed the habit becomes. Those actions that are repeated often enough so that they become strongly imprinted on your mind become *habits*; you do not need to think about them on a conscious level—they are automatic. Hence, your performance in the past controls your responses in the present and future, including both your physical and mental responses. Each player performs the way he or she does because of the physical (coordination) and mental (concentration) habits he or she has developed.

In short, skill is the product of mental and physical habits. Developing skill is something different, however; it involves feedback, which results from awareness. *Feedback through proper awareness is the key to developing correct mental and physical habits.* Feedback from your sense of body awareness is necessary to develop coordination, and feedback from your sense of mind awareness is necessary to develop concentration. Mind awareness is discussed in the next chapter, "Developing the Master Sense."

Using Body Awareness on the Court

You should use your heightened sense of body awareness in three situations—practice, warm-ups, and breaks in the game.

Body Awareness in Practice

During practice, you can use body awareness to develop shooting technique, to iron out moves and fakes, and to develop a shooting touch. In developing technique, moves, and fakes, you should use body awareness together with visual feedback. By rehearsing in front of a full-length mirror, you will receive immediate visual feedback indicating whether you are performing the movement correctly. (This is why ballet studios have full-length mirrors.) By closing your eyes and centering your attention on body awareness on every alternate rehearsal repetition, you will receive muscle feedback as well as visual feedback.

Getting the Feel. As a result of the combination of visual and muscle feedback, you will begin to know how your good moves *feel*, which is essential. When you play on the court, where there are no mirrors, you must operate by *feel* based on your sense of body awareness. There is no other way to perform with good fakes, moves, and proper shooting form. However, as you will see in the following chapters, your goal is not to center on body awareness when competing. The purpose of using body awareness in practice is for you to overlearn proper form and movements. By overlearning and developing habits, you will be able to play without centering on your sense of body awareness. Your moves will be *automatic* and controlled by your subconsious mind. Overlearning lets you center your attention on the visual cues presented during the game, information that is the key to success.

Shooting "Touch." Body awareness is the key to developing the fine "touch" and coordination of shooting. Shooting touch is developed by paying attention to how a good shot *feels.* You must increase your sense of body awareness if you wish to refine your shooting skill. By focusing on your sense of body awareness in practice you will polish your shooting mechanics and develop proper habits. Only then will you be able to progress to the next phase of learning—developing proper shooting concentration as discussed in chapter 5, "Shooting Fundamentals."

Body Awareness in Warm-Ups

In addition to practice, the pregame warm-up is a good time to focus on body awareness. When you first begin shooting in warm-ups, it is a good idea to center almost entirely on how your movements *feel.* Then as you loosen up and develop your shooting rhythm, gradually change your center of attention to your visual system and begin warming up mentally by maintaining your focus on the basket.

Body Awareness During Breaks in the Game

You can also use body awareness during breaks in the game. Any time there is a break in the action (i.e., a time-out, a free throw, a jump ball, or a change of possession with one team taking the ball out of bounds), take a moment to center on your muscles to detect any tension. If you feel tight, do not hesitate to use the tension adjustment exercises discussed in chapter 17, "Coping With Competition: The ABCs."

Summary

Skill is one of the critical factors of success in basketball. Players develop skill through a keen sense of body awareness. This provides muscle feedback enabling the athlete to distinguish successfully coordinated muscular responses from unsuccessfully coordinated ones. Body awareness is the key to developing skill.

One way to improve your sense of body awareness is through trampoline and balance beam training. Besides focusing on awareness in this special training technique, you should also use body awareness in practice, in warm-ups, and during breaks in the game.

Questions for Review

1. What is body awareness?
2. Why is body awareness important to an athlete?
3. What do we mean by muscle memory?
4. What is a habit?
5. What is the key to developing proper mental and physical habits?
6. When are some good times to use your sense of body awareness to improve your game?

Developing the Master Sense

> *But what then am I? A thing which thinks. What is a thing which thinks? It is a thing which doubts, understands, affirms, denies, wills, refuses, and which also imagines and feels.*
> —René Descartes (in Copleston, 1963, p. 104)

*T*he basic theme of this book is that basketball is as much mental as it is physical. Why is basketball as much mental as physical? Why are concentration, composure, and confidence so vital in attaining athletic excellence? The answer is simple: *Every movement of the body must be directed by the mind.* Whether you are shooting a basketball, hitting a baseball, or simply walking down the street, the mind directs the body in performing these "physical" tasks. The relationship between the mind and body is very close, and the activity or performance of the body is *always* the result of the processes of the mind. In other words, you must "use your head" in sport. The better your mind works in an athletic event, the better you perform.

If performance depends on the activity of the mind, then improving your performance is largely a matter of improving your mind. So the question now becomes, "How do you learn to control your mind during competition and practice?" The answer again is simple—through the power of *mind awareness*!

Mind Awareness

Imagine what it would be like to crawl inside a player's head to see what was going on inside as he or she performed (or failed to perform). Imagine bringing a video camera and recording everything you saw and heard. Just think how it would help that player to view a videotape of the images that passed through his or her mind during a game or practice. If this were possible, that player would be well on the way to achieving his or her potential on the court. With the videotape the athlete could see the appropriateness or inappropriateness of his or her thoughts for each game or practice situation. The mental feedback would be a tremendous learning aid. With it the athlete could control his or her mind to the best advantage.

Well, guess what? Whether you realize it or not, you can do just that. You can look into your own head, using the power of *mind awareness.* By developing mind awareness you can take control of your mental processes, and by taking control of your mental processes, you take control of your performance. In this way, mind awareness is truly the *master sense.*

Taking a Look Around Inside Your Head

Exploring your sense of mind awareness begins by considering the wide variety of thoughts that can attract your attention during practice or competition.

The Visual Field. First and foremost, a tremendous amount of visual information surrounds you. Your attention can encompass your entire visual field, which can be as wide as the largest arena holding fans, seats, scoreboard, players, coaches, cheerleaders, balls, baskets, benches, TV cameras, and so forth; or as narrow as only the ball or the rim. Your visual field can include the essential information for a particular play or unimportant objects such as an official or the ball boy.

Body Awareness. Second, your mind can focus on body awareness, through which you can sense muscle tension or relaxation. You can sense the rhythm or lack of rhythm in your coordination; you can sense sore or stiff muscles; you can sense high energy or fatigue; and you can sense the position of your body in space. In each of these cases your attention can be either very broad, taking in information from your entire body, or very narrow, focused on a specific body part or limb.

Your mind can also detect how balanced you are. If you are critically off balance, your mind focuses its entire attention on your equilibrium to enable you to regain control.

Sound.   Third, your attention can focus on the sounds of your environment. What you hear can be as broad as the roar of the crowd or as narrow as a teammate shouting, "Pick!" Focusing on sound can be essential, for example, when a teammate calls out a play; or it can be unimportant, as when the stadium organist plays.

Touch.   Fourth, your attention can center on touch. This focus can be as broad as the physical pressure of blocking out an opponent under the boards or as narrow as being slapped on the wrist while shooting. Your sense of touch can be essential, such as feeling your way through a pick; or it can be irrelevant, such as feeling your sweat-soaked uniform cling to your chest.

Mental Movies.   Fifth, you can be watching the movies in your mind—memories of the past or anticipation of the future. Mental movies can be positive, promoting confidence and composure; or they can be negative, prompting anxiety and tension.

Inner Voice.   Sixth, you can be listening to your own inner voice. Talking to oneself happens often, especially when things go wrong on the court.

Reflection.   Finally, your mind can be reflecting on itself and its own conscious attention. With this mental mirror, you can be aware of whether you have been focusing on your vision, hearing, balance, touch, body awareness, or imagination. You can even be aware that you are centering in mind awareness!

Keen awareness in each of these systems is occasionally useful or necessary. But too much attention to some systems distracts from the task at hand. The key to peak performance is learning to select the right focus of attention for a given game situation.

Selective Attention

There are many things on which your mind can focus during a game. However, as you remember from an earlier discussion, an ever-present psychological principle is at work in your mind. That is, while you are receiving information from each of your senses simultaneously, you can only focus your attention on one sense or one thought at a time. This sytem of selective attention, which we call *centering*, is the mental process of tuning in to one sensory system or thought channel while tuning out the others. For example, when you are centering on vision you are more aware of visual objects in your surroundings, but you are less aware of the sensations of hearing, touch, balance, or body awareness. You cannot be centering on two or more systems at the same time. As one system holds your attention, the other systems fade into the background of your mind. The best you can do is alternate your centering between systems.

When you have a broad focus of attention in any sensory system you are *soft centering*. Your mind perceives many things at once. A good example is when you are the ball-handler in the middle of a three-on-two fast break. Your vision is not focused on a particular object; it is focused on the entire playing area in front of you. A narrow focus of attention within a sensory system is called *fine centering.* An example of fine centering is when you are focusing solely on the basket when shooting. Although many other objects are in your field of vision, you are virtually oblivious to them. Your mind is only aware of one object, in this case the basket. Both soft and fine centering have their roles. You must learn on which form of centering to rely.

Using Your Mental Mirror

Mind awareness is the activity of the mind centering on itself. It is a "mental mirror" with a strictly internal focus of attention. As such, it is a very useful tool in developing basketball concentration skills. However, to use mind awareness you must rely on a mental memory for feedback on your mind's activity during the performance of a skill. According to the principle of selective attention (centering), when you are focusing on mind awareness, you are less aware of your other senses—vision, hearing, touch, and body awareness. Again, this is because the mind cannot center on two things at once. As one set of sensations or images moves into the center stage of your mind, the others fade into the background. Hence, when performing a skill like shooting that requires very specific visual information, you should be centering on vision and not on mind awareness or any of the other senses. As a result, you must rely on your mental memory for feedback on your mind's activity during the performance of a skill. The following exercises will clarify this point.

An Experiment in Mind Awareness

Begin by following the instructions below. Complete the required task before reading the question that follows.

1. Look out into the room in which you're sitting and focus your attention on your vision for about 10 seconds.

   While looking out into the room, did you soft center on the entire room or fine center on a particular object?

2. For the next 10 seconds, focus your attention on your sense of hearing.

    Were you aware of one sound in particular, or were you aware of several sounds coming from several directions?

3. Now center your attention on body awareness. If you are sitting, stand up. If you are standing, sit down.

    As you stood or sat, were you aware mostly of motion, the contraction of your muscles, pain, or stiffness?

4. For the next 10 seconds, let your mind focus on whatever it wishes.

    In which system and on what object did your mind focus?

The exercises you just performed practice *mind control* and *mind awareness*. In performing the tasks, you were practicing the art of mind control or concentration. In answering the questions that followed each task, you were using your sense of mind awareness. As you will see, these powers of mind are complementary. They are the keys to your basketball success.

Using Mind Awareness on the Court

You should use heightened powers of mind awareness in three situations—practice, warm-ups, and breaks in a game, just as you rely on body awareness at these times.

Mind Awareness in Practice.   In practice, mind awareness can be used to develop shooting, ball-handling, rebounding, and defensive concentration. In free moments between repetitions or during breaks between drills, take some time to reflect on your mind's focus of attention while performing those drills. Periodically during team drills and scrimmages, the coach should stop the action and ask players to reflect on their focus of attention.

Mind Awareness in Pregame Warm-Ups.   Pregame warm-ups are also good times to center periodically in mind awareness. When you first begin shooting in warm-ups, center almost entirely in body awareness. Then as you loosen up and develop your shooting rhythm, gradually change your center of attention to your visual system and begin warming up mentally by maintaining your focus on the basket. Use your sense of mind awareness to check your mental activity and to prepare for the upcoming competition.

Mind Awareness During a Game.   Mind awareness can also be used during breaks in a game to reinforce good habits. However, using mind awareness during competition should only be used as an occasional check. You should not dwell in mind awareness while playing because you will then have poor court awareness.

Attentional Style

Whether you are playing basketball, sitting in a classroom, driving a car, or engaging in any other activity, your mind is constantly bombarded with sensory data from your senses of vision, hearing, touch, body awareness, and balance. You can bring to mind a vast array of thoughts through recall and imagination as well. Where you center your attention results from one of two things. First, in a neutral or stable environment, your dominant thought channel (vision, hearing, touch, body awareness, imagination, inner voice, etc.) determines your selection of attention. However, when one set of impressions in your environment is more intense than others and thus demands your attention, your attention is dictated by the environment.

Reflect on this for a moment. If you have been sitting in a quiet room in a comfortable chair, relaxed but energetic, you probably have been centering almost entirely in your visual system, occasionally thinking about what has been discussed in this chapter. The less analytical you are, the more you centered your vision on the reading. The more analytical you are, the more you stopped reading to reflect on past experiences. In one case you are locked into vision. In the other case you strayed into your imagination. In both cases, your focus of attention was determined by your attentional style.

Conversely, if you are sitting at the kitchen table on a hard chair, hearing the television in the next room and rubbing your forehead because of a tension headache, your attention probably has been focused on the competing distractions and has switched rapidly from one disruptive thought to another. In this situation, regardless of your dominant thought channel, your attention was determined by the environment. It is important to note that your environment includes not only those things external to you but also your own body sensations and emotions; therefore, feelings of pain, fatigue, and emotional stress are environmental distractions.

In addition to having a dominant thought channel, you also have mental habits controlling the width of your attention within a sensory system. You may tend to fine center in your visual system or you may tend to soft center. Your particular type of dominant width of attention can be a blessing or a curse, depending on the situation or task at hand.

For example, if you have a dominantly visual, soft-centered focus of attention in which you focus on the entire court, you probably have developed the ability to hit the open player and help on defense. Yet because of this, you may have difficulty fine centering your vision on the basket when shooting. Your type of dominant mental focus prevents you from concentrating properly on your shot; therefore, you are probably a low-percentage shooter even if you have great form and mechanics. In situations where you have the opportunity to make a great assist on a clever pass, you look good. In situations where you must shoot from outside to "keep the defense honest," you're in trouble. But you *can* learn to adjust your focus.

Team Chemistry

The same principle of mental makeup also applies to teams. Much of the mysterious quality we call "team chemistry" can be attributed to the team's mental characteristics. An example of a "mental misfit" in a team's makeup is having a point guard with a dominant mental state of visual fine centering. A playmaker who is not in the habit of soft centering on the entire court will probably miss a lot of open teammates. His or her physical attributes may make the player an ideal point guard. But because his or her narrow focus of attention is better suited for shooting than playmaking, this player would probably be more valuable as a shooting guard.

Using another example, imagine a team having both guards oriented basically in body awareness. They are probably good drivers because of the moves they have developed through their keen sense of body awareness. On the other hand, they are probably poor outside shooters and playmakers because they lack the necessary soft-centered visual awareness. Against teams that play pressure player-to-player defense where it's easy to drive to the hoop, these guards look like All-Americans. But because they cannot shoot, they look like bums against opponents that sag and take away their drive.

Flexibility of Attention

Basketball requires a constantly changing focus of attention, so your attentional style must be flexible. Mistakes are made when flexibility breaks down. If your attention is inflexible you will be successful only in those situations that fit your style and relatively unsuccessful in situations that do not. To improve your chances of success you must develop visual flexibility. Repeat exercises like the mind control exercises described in this chapter. Also, you must become more aware of your attentional style and concentration as you practice the various fundamentals of offense, defense, and rebounding.

Developing Concentration

Developing concentration is similar to developing the complex coordination skills of shooting and ball handling. Awareness is the key! Developing and refining coordination require feedback from your sense of body awareness. Developing proper concentration requires feedback from your sense of mind awareness.

Two Sets of Habits

Because the skills of shooting, passing, dribbling, and receiving are actually a combination of concentration and coordination skills, two distinct but closely related sets of

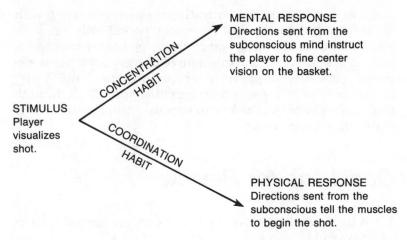

MENTAL RESPONSE
Directions sent from the
subconscious mind instruct
the player to fine center
vision on the basket.

CONCENTRATION HABIT

STIMULUS
Player
visualizes
shot.

COORDINATION HABIT

PHYSICAL RESPONSE
Directions sent from the
subconscious tell the muscles
to begin the shot.

Figure 4.1   Two types of practice habits are necessary for effective performance.

habits must be developed; one mental, one physical. Once developed, these habits must be made to work together. For example, when a player decides to shoot, the image of the shot in his or her mind (called the stimulus) triggers two responses—concentration (mental) and coordination (physical). See Figure 4.1.

Two Types of Practice

Figure 4.1 illustrates the necessity of two types of practice: one to develop concentration habits and the other to develop coordination habits. The two types of practice require two different types of awareness, mind and body. In the beginning, you must refine and strengthen your *coordination* habits (form and technique) by spending most of your practice time centering on *body awareness*. Once you master the body mechanics, you must refine your *concentration* through the use of *mind awareness*.

Summary

Mind awareness is the mind's ability to focus on itself. It provides you with feedback or a mental memory that tells you whether you are concentrating properly. By using your sense of mind awareness to reflect periodically on your mind's focus of attention you can develop proper concentration habits. Because the mind directs every athletic movement, you can improve your performance and bring consistency to your game by controlling your mind through mind awareness. As the key to success, mind awareness is truly the master sense.

Questions for Review

1. Why do we say basketball is as much mental as it is physical?
2. What is the master sense? Why?
3. What is mind awareness?
4. On what types of thoughts can your mind focus during competition?
5. When should you use your sense of mind awareness to improve your game?
6. What do we mean by attentional style?
7. What do we mean by flexibility of attention?
8. What type of attentional style is necessary for peak performance in basketball?
9. What is the key to developing concentration in basketball?

Second Quarter: Fundamental Skills

chapter 5

Shooting Fundamentals

Basketball is a mental game and this fact is probably more apparent in shooting than it is in any fundamental.
—John Wooden (1966, p. 84)

One of the goals of this book is to help you become a consistently good shooter. But shooting consistency is very difficult to acquire. Even for the game's great performers, the basket seems as big as a rain barrel some days and as tiny as a teacup other days. Although flaws in technique or other physical factors can contribute to inconsistency, the major reason is the inability to control concentration. This chapter will help you to develop and control your shooting concentration.

Rain Barrels Every Day

In order to be a consistently good shooter during games you must have both proper technique and concentration. You acquire proper technique through guided practice under the supervision of knowledgeable coaches and through the use of body awareness (see chapter 3, "Skill and Body Awareness"). Only when you have overlearned the proper motor coordination and have developed a natural rhythm of shooting can you learn to concentrate when shooting.

Concentration in shooting involves fine centering your vision on the target, enabling you to accurately judge the path the ball must take to go through the basket, and then letting your mind subconsciously direct your body in doing the rest. Being psyched out or "just having an off night" is a matter of poor concentration or not relaxing enough to follow through properly. Consistent shooting occurs when the Three Cs of peak performance are present.

Inappropriate Centering of Attention

Before discussing the necessary steps in developing proper shooting concentration, let's consider the several possible distractions affecting a poor shooter's concentration. For the sake of illustration, let's assume it's you who's having an off night.

If you are centering on your form and technique while shooting you are centering in the wrong sensory system (body awareness). If you are aware of body tension you are also centering in the wrong system (body awareness). If you are aware of being touched or fouled while shooting you are centering in the wrong system (touch). If you are off balance while shooting you are probably centering in the wrong system (balance). If you are aware of the fans or another player shouting at you when shooting you are centering in the wrong system (hearing). If you are wondering, "Will Coach think this is a good shot?" you are focused on your imagination instead of on your shot. If an opposing player comes flying at you trying to block your shot and you look at him or her instead of the basket, you are centering in the right system (visual) but on the wrong target.

Effective Centering of Attention

In other words, all your sensory systems can demand your attention when you are shooting, but you should be centering only on *one* distinct segment of your visual system. Your mind must be totally focused on the basket and nothing else. Mentally you must be visually absorbed by the basket. Physically and emotionally you must be relaxed and loose.

Sight Your Target. The first thing you must do when shooting is *sight your target*. You must fine center your vision on the basket as soon as possible. Coming off the dribble you must shift your focus of attention from soft centering on the action in front of you to fine centering on the basket. On receiving a pass you must quickly shift from fine centering on the ball to fine centering on the basket. Soft centering on the backboard is not enough. Shooting is a precise skill requiring fine centering. However, the target you use for bank shots is somewhat different than your target when shooting for the basket. When you shoot bank shots you must pick out the right spot on the backboard and maintain your focus on that point. You *must* fine center.

Mental Follow-Through. When shooting, you must follow through in concentration just as you must follow through in your arm extension. When you release the ball on your shot you must maintain your centering on the basket. *In no way should you follow the flight of the ball.* You should first see the ball when it comes into your field of vision about 2 feet above the rim. By maintaining your concentration on the basket, you avoid changing your focus of attention too early.

Five Stages of Development

In developing your shooting concentration you should be working through five stages:

1. Mental rehearsal
2. Body rehearsal (dry shooting)

3. Practicing by yourself with a ball
4. Developing your concentration in pick-up games
5. Utilizing shooting fundamentals in competition

Stage 1: Mental Rehearsal

In learning an athletic skill you must have a clear mental picture of the correct technique or form before you can do it successfully. This is where mental rehearsal comes in. Mental rehearsal is simply creating a mental picture or a series of mental pictures illustrating a proper technique or movement and the goal to be accomplished. Through mental pictures you instruct your body and mind on what you hope to achieve and how to carry out the necessary skills and movements. The more vivid and detailed the image, the better your mind and body can understand what they must do.

Using mental rehearsal to develop shooting concentration involves developing a clear picture of the target (the center of the basket) and the goal (putting the ball in the basket). It also involves developing a clear picture of *when* to focus on the target during the shooting movement (fine center on the target when you are bringing the ball up over your head just before releasing).

Begin mental rehearsal by stepping on a court and visually centering your attention on the backboard and rim. Develop a clear picture in your mind of the rim and backboard and then begin to fine center on the basket itself. See the front and back of the rim and all the hooks. Notice the contrast in perception here. When you are centering on both the backboard and rim you are soft centering. When you are looking specifically at the rim or the center of the basket, you are fine centering. This distinction of perception is crucial in order for you to become a good shooter.

The Center of the Basket. Because the goal of shooting is to put the ball through the basket, you must learn to fine center on the center point of the basket. This requires a clear mental picture of the *target* and the *goal*. Contrary to what many coaches and experts say, your shooting target is not the rim itself, the front of the rim, or the back of the rim. The true target is the center of the basket. By "basket," I mean the space within the circle of the rim. The exact target is the center point of this space. It is very important that you *learn to fine center on the center of the basket rather than simply soft centering on the backboard and rim when shooting.* You are awarded two points for putting the ball through the basket, not for simply hitting the backboard, rim, or net.

Close your eyes and imagine the rim in detail. Now narrow your attention to the center point of the basket as illustrated in Figure 5.1. Next, open your eyes and fine center on the basket, and then close your eyes again and form a clear mental picture of the basket and its center point. Do this several times. Then move around the court and look at the basket from many different angles and develop the same clear, mental picture. Do this again and again with your eyes open and then with them closed. Repeat this mental exercise until you have a vividly clear perception of your target (the center point of the basket).

Figure 5.1 Focus on the center point of the basket.

Programming for Success. Once you can fine center on the center point of the basket, you must develop a vivid picture of your goal—putting the ball through the hoop. Although this may seem elementary to some people, the ability to visualize achieving the goal distinguishes good shooters from poor ones and one player's good shooting performances from poor shooting performances. Good shooters *expect* their shot to go in. To them the goal is clear and positive. Poor shooters only *hope* that the ball will go in. The expected outcome, though often a subconscious thought, is at best unclear or at worst negative. Your next step in developing shooting concentration involves establishing in your subconscious mind, through conscious mental rehearsal, a clear and positive goal (putting the ball through the hoop).

To program yourself for success, begin by visualizing an imaginary ball going through the real basket. To get a vivid picture of a ball in your mind, take a basketball, hold it out in front of you, and notice all the detail you can about the ball. Now close your eyes and try to recreate the image in your mind. Open your eyes again and study the ball. Toss the ball up in the air with some backspin just as you do when shooting. Once again close your eyes and try to recreate in your mind this image of a ball with backspin. Repeat this exercise a couple of times until you can create in your mind a vivid image of a ball at will. Establish control of your image.

The next step in mental rehearsal is to walk around the court, fine center on the basket from different angles, and vividly imagine a ball about 1 foot (or one ball) above the rim and then falling through the basket. If the image of the ball begins to fade, look at the ball in your hand and recreate a vivid image in your mind. Now continue to visualize the ball going through the basket.

Once you have developed the habit of fine centering on the center of the basket you must learn to coordinate this skill with the body mechanics of shooting. Developing this ability is best achieved through body rehearsal.

Stage 2: Body Rehearsal

Body rehearsal is simply performing the body movements of a skill to develop a feel for them. Most athletes use body rehearsal methods in some form. Boxers shadowbox. Golfers, baseball players, and tennis players take practice swings. These rehearsals powerfully reinforce your muscle memory of the correct motions of a skill.

Body rehearsal should be used until a skill becomes automatic or second nature. Generally, when using body rehearsal practice methods, you are centering in the sensory system of body awareness. This focus of attention accelerates the learning of complex coordination tasks because of heightened muscle awareness. Once you have overlearned the body mechanics of shooting, you can also use body rehearsal to develop the mental mechanics of shooting until you overlearn those, too.

Because at this point we are only concerned with coordinating the concentration skills of visually fine centering on the center point of the basket with the body mechanics of shooting and not with actually making the shots, we can begin body rehearsal without a ball. This kind of body rehearsal is called *dry shooting*. The purpose of dry shooting *(w/out a ball)* is to eliminate anxiety over results so you can concentrate on coordinating the mental concentration skills with the body mechanics of shooting. Dry shooting helps you learn the physical sensations of shooting more efficiently because you are more aware of what your *body* is doing than what the ball is doing.

Now that you know the what, how, and why of body rehearsal, do it! Move around the court to various spots as if dribbling or moving to receive a pass and practice your shooting motion without a ball. When you begin to bring the imaginary ball up over your head to shoot, fine center on the center of the basket. After releasing the imaginary ball, imagine seeing it go through the basket to reinforce your positive expectations. Practice this drill until your visual concentration is so coordinated with your body mechanics that it becomes automatic or second nature.

Stage 3: Practicing by Yourself With a Ball

The next step in learning shooting concentration is to practice by yourself with a ball. In a noncompetitive environment, free from outside distractions, you will have no reason to be anxious about the results of your shots. You will have no one to impress with your performance. All you should be aware of is whether or not you are fine centering on the center point of the basket when you bring the ball over your head to shoot. *Learn to be aware of where you center* so you can properly adjust your attention. Remember, *awareness* is the key to controlling concentration.

When you first begin this concentration technique, you will find that you are inconsistent in your centering. Sometimes you will revert back to your old mental habits. When you miss a shot, ask yourself what you saw when you shot, what the object of your centering was. You probably did not fine center on the center point of the basket, and perhaps something else distracted you such as a loss of balance or awareness of body tension. When this happens make sure on your next shot that you fine center on the appropriate point. Reviewing your focus of attention on successful shots also helps to reinforce effective fine centering.

Another tip you should remember in practice is that after you miss a shot and see the ball hit the rim, falling long, short, or to the side, you must then *blot the image of the missed shot out of your mind and then visualize both the appropriate focus and the desired result—the ball going through the basket.* The reason for doing this is that you have a short-term visual memory, and if you shoot with the image of a missed shot in your mind, then your eyes will naturally tend to focus on where your last shot hit the rim instead of correctly on the center point of the basket. The image of the missed shot also reinforces a negative expectation rather than a positive expectation of the ball going through the hoop. This is why every time you miss a shot either in practice or in a game you must immediately replace the negative image in your mind (missed shot) with the correct positive image (swish!). You can do this during any break in the action, and soon positive expectation will become a natural habit for you to use in both practice and games.

Stage 4: Developing Your Concentration in Pick-Up Games

When your shooting concentration has become second nature, begin to use it in pick-up games and scrimmages. You may find that your centering is inconsistent when you first begin to use this technique in competitive situations. Informal competition in pick-up games or scrimmages increases the number of distractions you must overcome to concentrate on the basket. The primary distraction you must learn to ignore is the player guarding you, especially when he or she attempts to block your shot. However, even in scrimmages, highly competitive players can be distracted by anxiety over their performance. Rather than focusing on the basket when shooting, these players recall their past failures (missed shots). Competition affects your concentration at times and you must simply be aware of this when it happens. If you use your sense of mind awareness during breaks in a game, you can easily adjust your concentration as necessary so that you are centered on the right target (center point of the basket) for the next play. Occasionally using mind awareness during competition lets you control your concentration to your advantage.

Stage 5: Utilizing Shooting Fundamentals in Competition

The last step in learning to use shooting fundamentals is to try them in highly competitive situations—regular season games. Intense competition increases not only the variety of distractions (more so than pick-up games), but also the intensity of the distractions (including crowd noise, higher anxiety, etc.). Again, under these more stressful conditions, you may find yourself somewhat inconsistent at first in your centering; but your concentration will rapidly improve because you know what concentration is and can (through mind awareness) make the necessary adjustments when you are not centering properly.

Coaches' Corner

Specific in-season drills are not described here. You can devise your own drills to suit your situation. However, shooting drills should emphasize changes in visual centering. Some drills should require the shooter to change the focus of attention from fine centering on the ball when receiving a pass to fine centering on the basket when shooting. Other drills should require the shooter to change the focus of attention from soft centering on the entire court when dribbling to fine centering on the basket when shooting. Other drills can be devised to incorporate distractions that players must overcome. An example of such a drill is one in which a player must attempt to block the defender yet remain focused on the center point of the basket.

Summary

Now you know what shooting concentration is all about. All you need is the desire and determination to practice your shooting fundamentals. Remember, it takes hours and hours of practice to perfect this skill. However, when you master the mental basics and realize whether or not you are concentrating properly, you will easily be able to make the adjustment in concentration. At that stage you will be "on" much more consistently because you will be in control of your concentration.

Questions for Review

1. What two things does a player need to shoot consistently well?
2. Give some examples of poor concentration while shooting.
3. What is the first thing you must do when shooting?
4. Why is it necessary to follow through mentally?
5. What are the five stages to developing shooting concentration?

6. Where should your mind be fine centering when shooting?
7. What is dry shooting?
8. When you miss a shot, why should you blot the image of the missed shot out of your mind and then visualize the ball going through the basket?
9. How can competition affect your concentration? How can you prevent competition from affecting your concentration?

c h a p t e r 6

Shooting Slumps

Missing a few shots in a row is a normal occurrence for anyone who has ever played basketball. When a bad streak in a game is longer than usual, the player begins to press his shot. He begins to think about his technique and worry about the end result. Shooting is a simple, natural conditioned response. "Trying hard" at shooting complicates a very simplistic act. The antithesis of an uncluttered mind is a thoughtful mind. The good shooter should avoid "thinking" (like the plague), especially when the shots aren't dropping.
—*Stan Kellner (1978, p. 76)*

Every player has experienced a severe shooting slump at one time or another. Most players experience a couple of mild slumps each season. Few, however, know how to treat a slump. Many players react in a way that causes the situation to grow worse instead of better because they do not distinguish between a mistake and a flaw. A flaw is a defect in the mental and physical blueprint of shooting. A mistake is just a momentary lapse. Players who change their shot (the mental and physical blueprint) based on a mistake often increase a slump. They do not realize that the problem does not lie in their original shooting habits but rather in factors interfering with their established shooting habits. By changing their shooting technique to get out of a slump, players can often make the problem worse.

In this chapter we will look at how slumps start, how they continue and grow worse, and how a player can overcome them. By learning to handle a slump you will find the game much less frustrating and much more enjoyable.

How Slumps Start

Any time you miss a shot there is a reason for it. A missed shot results from a breakdown in the mental or physical execution of the act. Likewise, you fall into a shooting slump because of a breakdown in good mental or physical habits. For some reason your successful concentration and motor habits have been replaced with faulty habits. The newly acquired habits can be temporary, lasting only a few shots to half a game; or they can last for several games or even a whole season. The factors that trigger these changes in habit can be physical or mental.

Physical Factors

If you are physically tight at the beginning of a game because you did not warm up adequately or because you are anxious or nervous, you will not have the normal, smooth release that enables you to shoot well. As a result you will probably miss your first few shots. Usually, running up and down the court a few times reduces your physical tension and lets you loosen up. If, however, you become anxious about your performance and begin to think negatively, your muscle tension will remain at a high level and you will never relax enough to play well. Remember, just a little extra tension can throw you off; your muscles do not need to be tied up in knots for you to lose your touch.

Sometimes making one basket is enough to reduce your tension and return your confidence and touch. But often this isn't true, especially if you have already missed several shots. You may consider the shot you made as mere luck, and you're probably right. So you continue to play with high body tension and the resulting poor release.

Fatigue is another physical factor that can induce a slump. When you're tired, your muscles don't respond like they do when you're fresh. As a result, you're likely to be less accurate and to miss some shots. Because this usually occurs at the end of a game, you should be able to overcome the problem with rest and conditioning before the next game. However, if you let your physical problem *become* a mental problem because of performance anxiety, and you begin to doubt your ability, then you've initiated the downward spiral into a slump.

Mental Factors

In addition to the physical factors, four basic mental factors can initiate slumps. The ultimate mental cause of a slump is *poor visual awareness*. You must have a clear, precise goal in mind because shooting requires accuracy. If you are not fine centering on the center of the basket when shooting, your mind does not have the precise information it needs to complete the task successfully.

The second mental factor contributing to a slump is *negative thinking.* If you dwell in the past or anticipate the future, you are reducing your visual awareness of the present, specifically your awareness of the basket. In other words, thinking interferes with doing (shooting) because doing in the present relies on awareness of the present, not the past or future. The problem grows worse when you think negatively. Dwelling on past mistakes or worrying about what might happen increases body tension, which in turn disrupts coordination and prevents a smooth release.

A third cause of a slump is the *lack of a mental warm-up.* Just as you must loosen up physically, you must also loosen up mentally. If your mind focuses on past or future worries instead of present objects (basket, ball, etc.), you will start the game with your body receiving vague instructions from your mind. Your chances of success will be a matter of luck.

The final factor leading to a slump is *defensive pressure*. If your opponent is bigger or quicker than you are or is playing more intensely, your shot can be affected in two ways. First, you may tend to hurry your shot. As you quicken your release, you lose your shooting touch. Second, by forcing you to focus your attention on him or her instead of on the center of the basket, your defender has ruined your concentration. In either case, he or she has minimized your chances of hitting the shot.

The Downward Spiral

A basketball player's psyche is a fragile thing. One missed shot can set a player's mind plunging in a downward spiral toward sustained failure. Repeated misses accumulate to create an off night. The psychologically and emotionally immature athlete sees no end to the slump. Soon one off night leads to another, which leads to another. Not knowing the cause of the trouble, much less how to handle it, the slumping player becomes worried, frustrated, and desperate.

To understand this chain reaction of failure you must understand that shooting is an act performed through two sets of habits—one mental and one physical. A shot is missed because of poor visual awareness or poor technique. Either a player's visual habits and mechanics (proper form) are not adequately established to be consistent, or something interferes with their execution. Interferences might include visual distractions, fatigue, tension, or other factors. If the athlete begins to panic after several missed shots, new habits are established that become stronger with each miss.

For example, imagine you have been shooting very well during the past few weeks. But tonight you are playing in an especially critical game. Your anxiety over the outcome of the game and over your performance in front of a large crowd has created an unusually high degree of muscle tension. You do not overcome your extra tension during warmups, and as a result you are still tense on your first shot. Your tension in turn prevents you from following through properly. Your lack of follow-through forces you to throw up a brick. Throwing up a brick in front of several thousand fans increases your anxiety and muscle tension, and on your next shot you miss by an even wider margin. You begin to say to yourself, "Come on, jerk! You gotta hit the next one!" The pressure mounts. Your tension remains high, and your anxiety increases. On your next shot you let up a bit because your last two shots were long, only to throw an air ball.

Now you begin to panic and feel out of control. "Oh, man! What's wrong with me today? I can't hit a thing!" And so it continues. Your anxiety decreases for a moment as you hit one shot but it increases again as you miss the next one. Your confidence is shattered, and your only concern is for the half to end. In the locker room at halftime you are not even aware of your coach's comments as you dwell on your "bad luck" and think, "Maybe I'll get hot in the second half and save face."

This sequence is not uncommon. One mistake leads to another. The old habits of visually fine centering on the center of the basket and of shooting with a smooth, relaxed follow-through have been replaced by negative thinking (visualizing a missed shot as you release) and poor form with no follow-through. Your slump will continue as long as you continue to play with these new bad habits. The slump may continue for a game or two or for quite a while. How long a slump lasts depends entirely on how you handle it. With proper mind and body awareness, you can understand why you're in a slump and how to deal with the problem. Without awareness, you are a prisoner of your own bad habits until chance intervenes again and reestablishes your old habits of proper vision and smooth form.

Avoiding or Overcoming a Slump

If a slump is triggered by developing bad habits, avoiding a slump is as simple as avoiding bad habits. "But how do I avoid bad habits?" you ask. That's simple. Body and mind awareness are the only tools you need to maintain your form and concentration.

Whenever you miss a series of shots during a game, don't panic! Just take a moment at a break in the action to perform a quick mind and body check. First, consider your visual awareness on your shot attempts. Did you fine center on the center of the basket, or were you distracted? If you were distracted, imagine yourself shooting with the correct visual awareness; that is, focusing on the center point of the basket. This mental exercise should only take a second to perform.

Next, take a moment to center your attention in body awareness. Do you feel any tension? If so, perform the isometric tension-adjustment exercises described in chapter 17, "Coping With Competition: The ABCs." Then visualize your personal relaxation image. By performing these two exercises you will become more relaxed in a matter of seconds.

If you are already in the midst of a bad slump because you did not take any precautions, you must spend a little extra time practicing the physical and mental fundamentals. You must spend some time shooting while centering in body awareness to perfect your form and technique. In doing this you become reacquainted with your natural rhythm. You must also spend some time centering in mind awareness *after each shot* to reflect on your visual awareness. It is also a good idea to perform some dry shooting

(shooting without a ball) so that you are not distracted by anxiety over your progress.

Summary

Shooting slumps are a common occurrence that can be avoided and overcome by using body and mind awareness. You must also help yourself by not putting any additional pressure on yourself. Don't make more of a missed shot or an off night than it is. Pressure promotes negative thinking. Negative thinking creates anxiety and tension. These in turn produce poor concentration and tense muscles. The end result is newly developed, bad habits that you must overcome. In short, the best advice to avoid or overcome a slump is, *Be aware!* Use your powers of mind awareness and body awareness to keep your shooting touch.

Questions for Review

1. What causes a shooting slump?
2. What is meant by "downward spiral"?
3. How can a player in a slump start to panic?
4. What can you do to avoid a slump?
5. If you find yourself in a slump, what can you do to break out of it?

chapter 7

Free Throw Fundamentals

It takes extraordinary concentration after a player takes a "hard foul" not to show any signs of anger or frustration, at least momentarily. However, the player who disciplines himself and the one who knows and believes that TOTAL CONCENTRATION is the difference between success and failure at the line, will simply get off the floor, head to the top of the circle, and get ready to MAKE SOMEBODY PAY FOR IT!
—Bob Reinhart (1981, p. 28)

Next to the uncontested lay-up, the free throw is the easiest shot in basketball for obvious reasons. First, you always shoot a free throw from the same 15-foot distance. Second, you do not shoot on the move so you can be well balanced and set before shooting. Third, you do not need to hurry for fear of having the shot blocked; and finally, you have time to loosen up, develop your rhythm, and focus your vision on your target.

Making an Easy Shot Difficult

Although the free throw is normally an easy shot, it sometimes can become a very difficult shot; not because of the shot itself, but because of the pressure you add (see chapter 16, "Pressure and the Emotional Elements of Sports"). In a way, the extra time you have to prepare for a free throw can be as much of a disadvantage as an advantage. If you begin to think about the consequences of the free throw attempt, you create many problems for yourself. If you lack confidence or feel fearful, you create muscle tension and destroy your concentration. Your mind is not centered on vision; it is locked into the dark side of your imagination. The problem, then, is overcoming the pressures surrounding the task rather than the difficulty of the task itself.

Another problem you face in shooting free throws is the shooting slump. Sometimes you fall into bad habits and become inconsistent at the line. These slumps make the task more difficult by creating psychological pressure and eroding confidence. In short, you can make free throws the most difficult, easy task in the game.

Keeping Free Throws Simple

Shooting a successful free throw is best accomplished by having an uncluttered mind and a relaxed body. You must have proper visual awareness, loose muscles, and a rhythmic motion. When shooting a free throw, follow this routine every time:

1. *Loosen up.* Before stepping to the line, tense and relax your muscles to loosen them. Center your attention in body awareness as you perform the exercises to avoid distracting thoughts. As you step to the line, take a deep breath and exhale. Shake your arms slightly at your side while centering in body awareness.
2. *Practice body rehearsal/mental rehearsal.* At the line, take a moment to run through a body rehearsal routine of shooting with a good follow-through. Accompany this with a complementary mental rehearsal routine. Stan Kellner (1978) recommends developing the habit of shooting two mental free throws successfully in your mind. This is accomplished in a few seconds and produces a feeling of success.
3. *Get comfortable.* As you take the ball from the referee, readjust your feet until you feel comfortable. Bend at the knees to reduce the tension in your thighs and bounce the ball a few times if you like. Center in body awareness and get comfortable.
4. *Focus on the center of the basket.* Center your attention in your visual system and fine center on the center of the basket.

5. *Visualize success.* Just before shooting, visualize the ball going through the hoop to give your mind a positive image. *See an imaginary ball going through the real basket.*
6. *Do it!* You are ready, so get set, shoot, and follow through. Most importantly, don't think—just do it!

Make these six steps a part of your regular free throw routine, and you will have an uncluttered mind and a relaxed body and will keep a simple task simple regardless of the situation.

Practicing Free Throws

At the beginning of each season, shoot many free throws successively while centering in body awareness to develop good form (including relaxation) and rhythm. Next, practice shooting several free throws in a row using your sense of mind awareness to develop your concentration. As you near the first game and as the season progresses, shoot free throws in sets of two using the previously described routine before each free throw. When this routine becomes a habit you will have the two keys to shooting successful free throws—a relaxed body and an uncluttered mind.

Coaches' Corner

Learning to cope with pressure comes from experiencing pressure situations and applying relaxation/concentration techniques. Therefore, it is a good idea to simulate game pressure in practice. One way for coaches to do this is to finish practice by dividing players into teams with each player taking a turn to shoot "pressure" free throws. Begin by lining up all players on the baseline except the person shooting the free throw. If the player makes the shot the opposing team runs a sprint full court, down and back. If the player misses the shot, his or her team runs. The two teams alternate free-throw attempts until everyone has had a turn to shoot, or you may wish to continue the drill for a designated time period (such as 15 minutes). Opposing players may try to distract the shooter, thus adding to the pressure.

Questions for Review

1.   Why is a free throw an easy shot?
2.   What factors can make this easy shot difficult?
3.   Describe a routine that helps keep free-throw shooting easy.

c h a p t e r 8

Ball-Handling Fundamentals

The angle is what it's all about. I read the angles so that if I can hit that seam and find the angle, somebody can take the pass and shoot without breaking stride. It's just like shooting pool. You have to anticipate what's going to happen, read the angle, then POW! It just happens POW!
—Magic Johnson (in Newman, March 5, 1984, p. 5)

Steps, double dribble, wild, stolen, or fumbled passes—*turnovers!* The wide-open player alone under the basket, ignored and unseen—*another missed opportunity!* No wonder a coach's hair turns gray!

Are turnovers and missed opportunities physical mistakes? Are they due to poor technique? Think about it. Turnovers and missed opportunities rarely result from poor technique or coordination, especially on higher levels of competition. By the time a boy or girl has reached the high school varsity level, he or she has long since mastered the coordination and techniques of passing, receiving, and dribbling. Yet even on the college level turnovers occur on an

average of one every fifth possession. That seems like a lot considering the millions of times each college athlete has bounced, caught or thrown a basketball in his or her lifetime. Physical fundamentals are obviously not to blame, so the roots of the problem must be *mental*, specifically a lack of concentration, judgment, or composure.

Vision and Visualization

Basketball is a moving game. It is a game of constant action with most passes being made from one moving player to another or at least in situations where either the passer or receiver is moving. Add to this the movement of the defense trying to prevent a pass, and you have a constantly changing situation. As a result, quick judgment and anticipation are necessary; in fact, they are the crux of good ball handling. Anyone can pass to an open player when everyone is standing still. What distinguishes a good ball-handler is the ability to recognize when a player will be open and to pass him or her the ball at just the right instant, even when that player is moving. That takes visualization!

The great athletes, especially the great playmakers, have a keenly developed sense of anticipation. "There's something amazing about the way Magic can get it to you in traffic," says James Worthy of Magic Johnson, the NBA's premier playmaker (Newman, March 5, 1984, p. 15).

Visualization, which may best be described as a combination of vision and imagination, is the basis for judgment and anticipation in athletics. Visualization tells the passer where to pass the ball to hit a moving receiver and tells the receiver how to fake and where to move to get open for a pass. Visualization tells the dribbler which way to cut, which direction to drive, where to slow down, and where to stop and pivot.

Locking Into Vision

The ability to visualize well involves the mind's ability to lock into the visual system. When your concentration is diverted to unimportant messages from other sensory systems (such as a loss of balance, high body tension, the roar of the crowd), the visual input to your mind decreases dramatically and "things seem to happen too fast." But when your mind remains tuned in to your visual system and you calmly and clearly see the entire court in front of you, "time seems to slow down" as if you are watching the action in slow motion. Any ball-handler who maintains visual concentration and composure more than doubles his or her power of visualization. In this situation, judgment is not only quicker but also more accurate so that you can utilize opportunities and eliminate errors.

A good example of disrupted visual concentration is a loss of balance. If a loss of balance demands your attention, your vision and visualization partially disengages from seeing and anticipating. Your vision forfeits the task of passing to the more immediate task of regaining balance. As a result your muscles receive many kinds of contradictory messages, and your actions reflect this. Your mind is partly on passing and partly on regaining balance so you do not fall. In this extreme situation, the pass—if there is one— will probably miss its target.

Preconditions for Good Vision

Proper vision has a few requirements. First, you must have proper footwork when dribbling, receiving, or passing so you do not lose your balance as in the preceding example. John Wooden claims that proper footwork is the foundation of all the fundamentals. "Footwork is the most essential part of every fundamental because it is necessary for body balance and very little can be accomplished without balance" (Wooden, 1966, p. 124). Proper footwork must be overlearned; that is, it must be executed subconsciously through force of habit.

Second, you must overlearn the proper coordination of dribbling and passing so you do not need to focus on body awareness for correct execution. If your mind is focused on your body, your awareness of the court is necessarily reduced.

Third, you must learn to control your dribble and maintain control of the ball through touch instead of vision; such fingertip control must become automatic. A player who watches the ball cannot possibly see the entire court, too. If your mind focuses on your hand touching the ball, it loses visual awareness. The great ball-handlers can control their dribble through "subconscious touch."

Fourth, you must be in top condition to maintain your concentration. Fatigue detracts from your vision by forcing you to center on your tired body instead of on the open player.

Finally, you must be able to maintain your composure. You must feel self-confident so that distracting emotions do not ruin your concentration. A player who does not have faith in him- or herself will find his or her imagination (in the form of fears, anxieties, anger, and frustration) running off with his or her visual concentration. You must remain mentally relaxed by employing positive thinking and physically relaxed by using relaxation techniques.

Court Awareness

Because basketball is a fast-moving game of constant action, you must be aware of everything around you. Once you are aware of the situation, you must summarize it and notice any significant changes in it so you can respond properly. This means you must have a broad focus of attention (except when receiving or shooting) and let your mind touch everything evenly—teammates, defenders, and their relative position to one another. Court awareness is largely the result of *visual soft centering.*

Passing

The importance of passing cannot be overstated. Without passing, there would be few good shots because most good shots are set up by a succession of passes. To make the *right* pass in a given situation you must see the entire court so you know where the openings are. To make a *good* pass you must see where the potential receiver is going and spot any potential interceptors at the same time. You must judge the angle of the pass and anticipate. Passing skill requires visual *soft centering.*

You do not need to fine center as much on your passing target (the receiver's hands or chest) as you do on your shooting target (center of the basket). Passing does not require the same precision as shooting; the shooting target is generally much smaller than the passing target. If you feel you must fine center your vision to "thread the needle," it is probably not a high-percentage pass. Second, the basket is a stationary target, whereas the receiver can move and make adjustments to compensate for a slightly off-target pass. Finally, a player who is visually soft centered is less likely to telegraph passes with his or her eyes.

Receiving

Receiving has two phases. The first is getting open. To get open you must spot an opening, outmaneuver your defender by faking and reacting to your defender's actions, keep an eye on the passer, and be aware of other teammates helping to free you with a pick. This phase requires visual *soft centering.*

The second phase, catching the ball, is a hand/eye coordination task requiring total concentration on the ball. There is little room for error when receiving. This means you must quickly adjust your concentration from soft to *fine centering* as the pass is being delivered. Once you catch the ball you must immediately refocus your attention. If you are going to shoot, you must shift from fine centering on the ball to fine centering on the basket. If you're going to pass or haven't decided what to do yet, you must shift from fine centering on the ball to soft centering on the entire court to make your decision. Drills 3, 4, 5

Dribbling

Whether you are standing and holding the ball or advancing it on the dribble, passing to the open player requires proper visual awareness. You cannot see what is happening around you if your head is down and you watch the ball as you dribble. You must be able to dribble with your head up and be visually aware of everything occurring around you. Soft centering your vision on the action while dribbling means you must control the ball by touch on a subconscious level. Only when you *feel* a loss of control should you actually look at the ball. Whenever you practice dribbling, practice with your head up. Use the visual control drills described at the end of this chapter.

Visual Flexibility

In basketball you should not maintain a constantly narrow or broad focus of attention. Sometimes you must fine center, and other times you must soft center. Because basketball is such a fast-moving game with little time to think things through, it is critical that you are able to change your attention instantly from one focus to the other. You must develop the mental habits of fine centering your vision when shooting or catching the ball and of soft centering your vision for most other offensive situations.

A good example of the necessity of visual flexibility is the situation in which you are dribbling up the middle on a three-on-two fast break. As you approach the free throw line, you must assess the situation. You must react to what the defense does. If one defensive player comes out to guard you, one of your teammates is open and you must not only be able to see him or her, but you must also see the other defensive player and everyone's position relative to the basket. Only by being aware of the total situation can you visualize correctly and determine the fake you should use before you pass, which technique you should use, and where to pass the ball. This requires a broad focus of attention. If you are visually centering on the defensive player guarding you, your focus of attention is too narrow and you are unable to see the open player. Or if you focus only on your teammate and do not see the other defensive player, you may make a pass that is easily deflected or intercepted. Again, *soft centering* when passing is crucial.

However, remember that when you decide to shoot you must instantly narrow your focus of attention and fine center on your target—the center point of the basket.

It cannot be said often enough: Basketball requires visual flexibility. Practice the visual control drills on soft and fine centering. Many practice drills that require you to change instantly from soft centering to fine centering and vice versa are listed in chapter 15, "Mind Games," and at the end of this chapter. Many drills also focus on the ability to shift attention instantly from one object to another object. For example, one drill may require you to fine center on the ball while receiving a pass or rebounding on the offensive board and then immediately fine center on the rim to shoot.

Although all players should develop their court awareness and visual soft centering skills, this is an *absolute necessity* for the play-making guard. Not only must the playmaker be visually soft centered, that player must also be mentally active and anticipatory, looking for the open player. He or she cannot react passively and slowly to openings. As the primary passer, the playmaker is an important element of any team.

The good play-making guards have generally developed visual awareness that is predominantly soft centered. However, this type of visual dominance has both advantages and disadvantages. As a play-making guard, soft centering makes you an effective initiator of the offense. Yet, if you have not developed the habit of shifting your focus of attention to fine centering on the center point of the basket when shooting, you will not contribute as effectively to the offense as you might. Your shooting efforts will suffer.

Coaches' Corner

Most of the floor drills described here are in-season team drills, though some may be used by individuals in the off-season as well. During these drills players have the opportunity to apply their developing concentration skills.

Dribbling Drills

The key to effective dribbling is being able to maintain visual awareness of the entire court while controlling the ball by touch. The following drills are designed with this in mind.

Dribbling Drill 1—Blind Man's Bounce. Because dribbling is enhanced by fingertip control, close your eyes and fine center your attention on the touch sensitivity of your dribbling hand. As you bounce the ball, notice where your hand makes contact with the ball. Your palm should not touch the ball. Keep bouncing the ball until you feel only your fingertips coming in contact with it. Do this drill first with one hand and then with the other. Next, vary the force of the dribble. Feel the difference between pounding the ball on the floor and lightly bouncing the ball. This drill is excellent for learning fingertip ball control.

Dribbling Drill 2—Dribbling Rhythm. Again, keeping your eyes closed, dribble the ball in front of you or at your side. This time, however, center your attention on your dribbling arm. Focus your attention on body awareness and feel the rhythm and movement of your arm. Vary the height of your dribble from 2 inches off the floor to shoulder height. Your overlearned coordination of dribbling acquired through body awareness aids your sense of touch in controlling the ball without watching it. Your vision is then free to spot the open player.

Dribbling Drill 3—Change-of-Pace Dribbling. Practice both low dribbling (for control) and high dribbling (for speed) while soft centering on the court, fine centering on an object, and shifting the focus of your attention from soft centering to fine centering and vice versa.

Dribbling Drill 4—Dribble King. In an area about one-fourth of the court, each player must attempt to steal or deflect the ball away from the other players while also dribbling. The last person left standing with control of his or her dribble wins. This drill requires each player to maintain the dribble by touch, protect the ball with the body, soft center on the entire court to be wary of attackers from all sides, and switch attention to fine centering when attacking another player's dribble.

Dribbling Drill 5—Dribble War. In this drill the area of battle is increased to half of the court, and players are divided into two teams. The team that stops the dribble of each of the opponent's players wins.

Passing and Receiving Drills

Passing and receiving drills in which two players play catch while standing still with no defenders are useless except on the elementary level. Turnovers occur when there is difficulty in perception because either the passer or receiver or both are moving. Because of this, passing and receiving drills should have movement. They should also emphasize visual flexibility, requiring both visual soft centering to move to the open area and also a sudden shift to fine centering on the ball when it is being caught. Receivers commit turnovers because they do not make this mental transition effectively. Turnovers also occur because the passer often "underperceives." That is, he or she sees only the receiver and not the defenders. The player fine centers on the target so that he or she is unaware of defenders, even though they are in the field of vision. To develop soft centering skills, passing and receiving drills should include defenders, forcing the passer to soft center and to make quick decisions along with mechanical, physical responses.

Passing/Receiving Drill 1—Three-Player Weave. The three-player weave drill is an excellent drill for developing passing and receiving skills. Players form three lines at one baseline. The players in the middle line begin with the ball. The first player in each line works with the first player of the other two lines. They pass the ball to one another while running a weave pattern the full length of the court. To form the weave, the ball-handler in the middle lane passes to the next player cutting to the middle. After making the pass the passer cuts behind the receiver and replaces him or her in

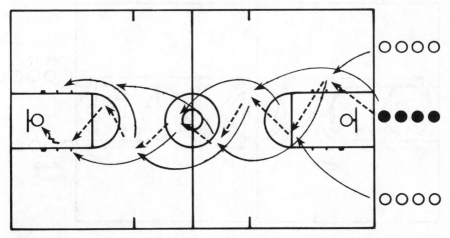

Figure 8.1 Passing/Receiving Drill 1—Three-Player Weave.

the outside lane. The receiver becomes the middle player and immediately passes to the opposite wing cutting to the middle. This pattern continues until one player is close enough to shoot a lay-up. After making the lay-up, the three players must jog back to the starting baseline to get in line for their next turn. Players should use the bounce pass one time down the court and the chest pass the next time. The weave is illustrated in Figure 8.1.

Passing/Receiving Drill 2—Double Trouble. In this drill (see Figure 8.2), players form two lines at one baseline with one line on each side of the free throw lane. All players have a basketball. The players in one line match up with a partner in the other line. The drill begins with the first set of partners passing two basketballs back and forth to one another while running the full length of the court. When one set of partners reaches the free throw line, the second pair begins. To prevent passes from colliding with one another, one partner throws all bounce passes while the other partner throws two-handed chest passes. Thus one pass is thrown low and the other is thrown high. When all players reach the opposite baseline the drill repeats in the opposite direction, only this time the partner who threw the bounce passes now uses the chest pass and vice versa. This drill is excellent for developing quick, physical reactions and the ability to shift quickly from fine centering on the ball when receiving to slightly softer centering on the receiver when passing.

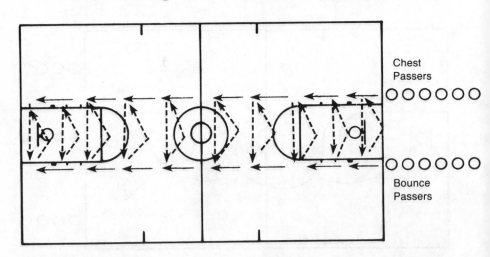

Figure 8.2 Passing/Receiving Drill 2—Double Trouble.

Passing/Receiving Drill 3—Monkey-in-the-Middle. In this drill, two offensive players stand on opposite sides of the free throw lane. They are not permitted to move. The passer is pressured by a defender—the monkey-in-the-middle—who crowds the passer and tries to deflect the pass (see Figure 8.3). In order to make the pass, the passer must fake the defender to create an opening. If the pass is completed, the receiver must wait until the middle player moves across the lane to apply pressure before a return pass can be made. Every 30 seconds one offensive player changes places with the "monkey." This is an excellent drill for passers to learn to cope with tight one-on-one pressure.

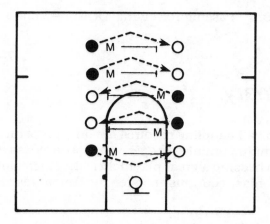

Figure 8.3 Passing/Receiving Drill 3—Monkey-in-the-Middle.

Passing/Receiving Drill 4—Monkeys-in-the-Middle. This drill is similar to the one above except there are three offensive players and two monkeys-in-the-middle. One offensive player is positioned at the middle of the free throw line, and the other two offensive players stand one step off the blocks. The middle player closest to the ball must attack the passer and try to deflect the pass. The other middle player must attempt to steal the pass made to one of the receivers. Every 30 seconds two offensive players change places with the two monkeys. This drill, shown in Figure 8.4, is similar to the game of "keep away" and is excellent for developing the passer's ability to cope with pressure and to spot the open player.

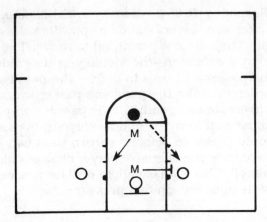

Figure 8.4 Passing/Receiving Drill 4—Monkeys-in-the-Middle.

Summary

Good ball handling requires not only proper mechanics and technique but also proper visual awareness and flexibility. To become a great playmaker like Magic Johnson or Isiah Thomas, you must master the fundamentals of ball handling.

Questions for Review

1. What is visualization?
2. Why is visualization important in ball handling?
3. What is the key to visualization?
4. What are four preconditions for good vision?
5. What is the proper type of centering for passing?
6. What is the proper type of centering for moving into position to receive the ball?
7. What is the proper type of centering for catching the ball?
8. What is the proper type of centering for dribbling?
9. What is visual flexibililty? Why is it important in ball handling?

chapter 9

Defensive Fundamentals

> *While it is important to put points on the scoreboard, it is just as important to stop the opposition from scoring. All good teams put as much stress on defense as they do on offense. . . . So much of defense depends upon one's attitude. Consequently, anybody can become a good defensive player if he puts his mind to it.*
> —Gail Goodrich (1976, p. 25)

Any discussion of defensive fundamentals must begin with the importance of attitude. Winning basketball begins with the realization that defense, along with offense and rebounding, is one of the three major elements of the game. Preventing your opponent from scoring means as much to the final outcome as does scoring an equivalent amount of points yourself. You must be eager, not just willing, to play defense.

Coaches generally believe defense is the *most consistent element* of the game. If you are physically capable of playing good defense, you are capable of playing good defense every night, because defense requires much less skill than offense. On defense you do not need to manipulate the ball; just get it. Concentration and intensity, then, are the most important aspects on defense. If you work and concentrate, you most likely will do well. Then on an evening when the offense suffers from poor execution, you can still save the game if you play good defense; if you do not play tough defense, the game is lost unless your offense is successful. Great players and great teams rely on tough defense to help them through the off nights.

Taking the Initiative

Any book that discusses defensive basketball also emphasizes the need to play aggressively and to take the initiative on defense. This emphasis reflects the defender's inherent disadvantage. A defender must react to the offensive player's moves. The offensive player has many options and knows what he or she will do. Your primary job on defense (and your only hope) is to eliminate some of those options and force the offensive player into less advantageous situations. You do this only by taking the initiative yourself. Pete Newell, one of the game's great coaches, says:

> It is a good idea to preach initiative on defense. The man with the ball and the defensive man attempting to guard him are, or should be, waging a physical and mental battle. Too often defensive men are taught just to react to the offensive man's moves and fakes. If the defensive man initiates motion in this battle between the two men he will have the offensive man reacting to his moves and fakes. The man who takes the initiative usually has the advantage as he has his opponent reacting to him. . . . In a sense, this initiative is the sum total of alertness, determination, anticipation and aggressiveness. This quality can't be emphasized enough. It can be the difference between fair, good, or great defensive men and teams. (Newell & Bennington, 1962, p. 255)

Defending Your Player Before He/She Gets the Ball

Taking the initiative on defense means playing the offense tough *before* that player receives the ball. Do not wait until he or she has the ball to become aggressive. Today's players are so skillful on offense that a defender can hardly prevent a good offensive player from taking a good shot in a one-on-one situation. Yet many defenders wait until their player receives the ball before playing defense, for a few reasons.

"No Ball, No Problem!" The primary reason for the lack of intensity in guarding a player without the ball may be the attitude that, "If my player doesn't have the ball, how can he [or she] score?" The problem with this attitude is that if you do not work hard to deny your opponent the ball, sooner or later he or she *will* get the ball and probably in an advantageous position. Then you're in trouble.

"Saving Energy."   Perhaps this attitude is reinforced by a second faulty perception that, "Because my player doesn't have the ball, I can relax and rest up for offense until the time when my player does have the ball and I must play tough against him [or her]." The problem with this approach of saving energy when your player does not have the ball is, again, that sooner or later your player will receive the ball where he or she wants it, in an advantageous situation. Because good team defense requires pressure on the ball and *help* from teammates, even when your player does not have the ball you must be ready at all times to *deny* your player the ball and to *help* a teammate who has been beaten.

Selfish Defense.   Finally, selfishness prevents some players from playing defense with 100% effort, even though most players realize that defense is essential to winning. The selfish player's main goal is not team success but individual scoring honors. The selfish player saves energy for offense. In another sense, some players also play selfish defense by focusing all their energy on stopping "their" player, so they are less apt to help their teammates when necessary. In both cases the player may perform well individually but reduces the defensive effectiveness of the entire team. Any player who is not primarily concerned with doing everything possible to help the team win is, by definition, a loser.

When you think about it, your player has the ball on average only one fifth of the time that you are playing defense. This suggests that defense is mostly a matter of denying your player the ball and providing defensive help; how can you consider not giving your best effort just because *your* player does not have the ball? To give 100% on defense you must be ready to do your job whether or not your player is an immediate scoring threat.

Defensive Strategies

In addition to attitude, defensive strategies are also important. One of the best individual defensive strategies is to deny your player his or her favorite spots and to capitalize on his or her weaknesses based on your knowledge of the opponent.

Deny Favorite Spots. Before discussing defensive concentration, one final point is necessary. Most players like to receive the ball and shoot from particular spots on the floor. When they receive the ball where they want it, when they want it, and are allowed to shoot from their favorite spots, they become confident and almost worry free. When you deny your player both the ball and that favorite spot, you take away confidence and leave him or her frustrated. In fact, nothing is more frustrating for an offensive player than a defender who prevents movement to preferred positions on the floor. No one likes to play against a good defensive team or player because it is so frustrating. If you want a psychological edge, deny your opponent his or her favorite spot.

Knowledge of Opponent. Knowledge of your opponent is very helpful on defense. Knowing what he or she can and cannot do, as well as what your opponent likes to do, is very useful. This information enables you to anticipate possible moves and to take the initiative. By studying your opponent carefully and using mental rehearsal techniques, you can keep one step ahead of your player. (See chapter 18, "Pregame Programming and Postgame Analysis.")

Defensive Concentration

Good defense requires properly focused, sustained concentration. For the most part your mind should be focused on your visual system. However, you must also be receptive to cues acquired through hearing and touch. Equally important, you must overlearn the proper defensive stance and footwork. Your senses of balance and body awareness will not demand your attention if you have overlearned the fundamentals of the defensive slide. Finally, body tension and fatigue can be controlled and prevented from interfering with your defensive concentration through proper conditioning and relaxation techniques (see chapter 17, "Coping With Competition"). The rest of this chapter describes each of these important aspects of defense.

Visual Awareness

Your visual awareness on defense varies with the situation depending on whether you are playing off the ball, guarding a player before the dribble, guarding the dribbler, or guarding a player after he or she has dribbled.

Off the Ball. As Pete Newell says, "Good vision implies good defense. A defensive man's vision under all circumstances should encompass the ball and his [or her] assigned opponent" (Newell & Bennington, 1962, p. 252). If this is true, your vision should be soft centered most of the time you play defense because four fifths of the time your player does not have the ball. If you are centered only on your player, your area, or the ball, you have poor visual awareness. This hurts your team because you will react slowly to situations developing outside your focus of attention. You will probably not be in a position to help a teammate when necessary.

Proper vision is strongly correlated to proper positioning. If your vision encompasses your area, player, and the ball, you are probably positioned properly. To ensure the proper width of attention, a helpful defensive rule to apply when your player does not have the ball is to keep one hand pointing toward the ball and the other hand pointing toward your player. This is your area of interest. If your vision is properly soft centered, you will be more apt to intercept passes, recover loose balls, assist teammates, and defend against opponents left uncovered near the basket. However, you must be ready to change your focus instantly to fine centering when you are reaching for a loose ball or intercepting a pass.

Before the Dribble. When your player has the ball and has not used the dribble, you should fine center your vision on his or her stomach. Do not fine center on the eyes, feet, or ball; you will be susceptible to fakes. An offensive player can fake with the head, shoulders, feet, or ball but cannot go anywhere without his or her midsection.

Guarding the Dribbler. When your opponent is dribbling, keep your head directly between the ball and the basket. Your vision should be fine centered on the ball. This helps you maintain proper position on your player and enables you to deflect or pressure the ball with your hands.

After the Dribble. If your player has picked up his or her dribble, you should fine center your vision on the ball and use your hands to put on pressure. By following the ball with your vision and hands you have a good chance of deflecting a pass.

Visual Flexibility

A good defensive player, like a good offensive player, is able to change his or her focus of attention at will. The type of concentration used for a particular situation depends on whether the opponent is dribbling, holding the ball before dribbling, holding the ball after dribbling, or playing off the ball. Each situation demands a different focus of attention that must be practiced until it is overlearned and becomes a mental habit.

Anticipation

Pressure and help are the two vital elements of sound defense. Physical quickness enables you to achieve the first element, but only *mental* quickness can guarantee the latter. Defensive help requires *quick anticipation* and *reaction* as the offense may create a one-step advantage on the defense by initiating an action while the defense reacts to the initiative. To make up this deficit the defense must *anticipate*. Anticipation is a mental first step that is achieved only through visualization. To intercept a pass, block a shot, take a charge, or otherwise cut off a driver or cutter, you must anticipate. This requires visual awareness (see chapter 12, "Quickness").

Hearing and Touch

A good defense is always a *talking* defense. However, talking accomplishes nothing if no one is listening. A team that talks and listens on defense increases every individual's court awareness from 180° to 360°. You may be unable to see what is happening behind you, but you can hear what is happening if someone is talking. For example, you can avoid a screen if you are forewarned. Good communication also enhances anticipation, which again is the crucial, mental first step.

Using your sense of touch is also a clever way to increase your defensive awareness. For example, when guarding a player in the low post, you can keep track of him or her by using your sense of touch. By using touch you remain aware of the rest of the court through visual soft centering. Another example is using your sense of touch to fight through a blind side screen. In this situation you can use your hands to feel for the player who is screening so that you can visually focus on your player at the same time. If you turn around to look for the screen, you will probably lose sight of your player.

Intensity

Defense does not require the same skill level or fine coordination as offense does. It does require total physical exertion and aggressiveness. Hence, the proper level of intensity on defense is almost an all-out effort. This high-level intensity is necessary to dominate your player defensively (see chapter 11, "Intensity").

On a scale of 1 to 10, with 1 being total relaxation and 10 being an all-out effort, defending your player when he or she has the ball requires a "9" level of intensity. In this situation your vision should be focused only on your player and your adrenaline should be pumping. When your player does not have the ball, you should relax slightly to an "8" level and soft center your vision on the entire action. But you must always be ready to help and to switch back instantly to a "9" level of intensity when necessary.

Conditioning

To play at such a high level of intensity requires tremendous conditioning. You must dedicate yourself to hard work and program yourself for high intensity on defense. Because defense requires much lateral movement and quick starts and stops, you must be willing to work hard during defensive drills designed to increase lateral quickness and stamina.

Off-Season Practice

Players can develop defensive concentration and intensity during the off-season as well as during the playing season. A dedicated player interested in improving his or her game does not need a coach's prodding to concentrate and to play hard. Self-motivation is every player's responsibility.

During the off-season you can practice defensive concentration while playing one-on-one or pick-up games. When playing one-on-one you use and develop the various types of concentration necessary for defending your player when he or she has the ball. In pick-up games, whether they are two-on-two or five-on-five, you can develop your visual flexibility, changing your focus of attention from fine centering to soft centering to meet the game situation.

Coaches' Corner

Defense is played primarily with the head and feet. Thus defensive drills should be designed to improve the use of the mind and footwork, such as drills in which players must focus their attention on body awareness to develop stance, slide, and quickness of foot; and drills in which they use various types of concentration, including soft and fine centering. Remember, skill involves practice, not just awareness. To play successfully players must practice until their actions become habits, and you must *drill for skill*.

There are seven basic types of *in-season drills* that a coach should use in every practice to sharpen and to reinforce the proper focus of attention for each of the primary defensive situations.

Defensive Stance: Focus on Balance

Developing star defensive players begins by teaching proper balance. Balance comes naturally when using the correct stance. Players must learn how the proper stance *feels*. The basics of proper defensive balance include the following:

- Feet should be slightly more than shoulder width apart.
- Weight should be on the balls of the feet.

- Knees should be bent.
- The butt should be down and the back straight.
- The head and chin should be up.
- Arms should be spread with one held high and the other low.

As your players assume the defensive stance, instruct them to focus their attention on balance and body awareness and on how the correct stance feels.

Developing Quick Feet

After learning the proper stance, players must be taught to use their sense of body awareness to learn the *feel* of the defensive slide. Developing a smooth, natural rhythm of movement is important. However, this movement is not a slow rhythm; it is very quick. So once your players have learned the smooth, gliding motion, instruct them to center their attention on their feet. They must force their feet to move faster by quickening the rhythm, without sacrificing balance or control. During defensive slide drills, remind your players to pay attention to foot speed, not fatigue. Between drills and even during drills, ask them to imagine their feet moving faster. Soon their feet will be catching up with their imagination. (See chapter 14, "Suggestology and Mental Rehearsal: Easy-Chair Drills" for a discussion of how to use mental rehearsal to improve your foot speed.)

Get the Feel. To help your players develop a clear image of quick feet, ask your quickest player to demonstrate the defensive slide for the others. Instruct the slower players to imagine their feet moving at the same speed as the quick player's feet. They should picture their feet in his or her shoes and "feel" the quick movement of the feet.

Drill 1—Defensive Slide. Before this drill begins, the coach should emphasize the use of body awareness and should correct incorrect stances. As shown in Figure 9.1, a team of 12 members lines up in three rows of four players for defensive sliding following the coach's commands (left, right, forward, back). Players should focus their attention on the rhythm of their slide and the quickness of their feet. Using their imagination, players must "think" their feet quicker.

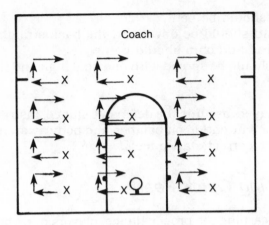

Figure 9.1 Drill 1—Defensive Slide.

Once players have developed quick feet and have over-learned the defensive slide, their focus of attention must shift from their body and feet to their other senses—vision, hearing, touch. Incorporate drills into your practices that emphasize each of these senses. Because vision is the most important we will begin with it.

Pressuring-the-Ball Drills

Guarding the player with the ball requires visual fine centering. Players must focus on the ball if their player is dribbling or has used up the dribble. Or they must focus on his or her midsection if he or she still can use the dribble. Because the defender faces three different situations, he or she must perform three different types of defensive drills. One type must require players to fine center on the ball while guarding the dribbler. Another type must require them to pressure the player who has lost the dribble; and another must require them to fine center on the midsection of the player who still has the dribble to use.

Drill 2—Guarding the Dribbler. Before beginning this drill, coaches should emphasize visual fine centering on the ball. If quick feet and a natural slide have been overlearned, the defensive player can focus his or her attention on the ball. He or she can then try to deflect the ball by reaching *up* with the hands (bringing the hands up from the floor). This drill

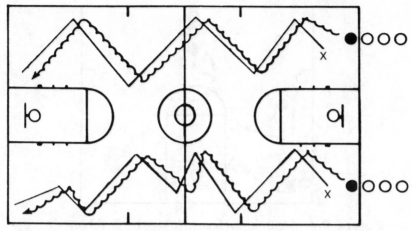

Figure 9.2 Drill 2—Guarding the Dribbler

can be done either by having the dribbler zigzag full court and change direction within a 12-foot wide area, or by having the dribbler start from one of the primary offensive areas (point, wing, corner) and drive toward the basket. Defenders stay with the dribbler and try to deflect the ball (see Figure 9.2).

Drill 3—Defense Before the Dribble. Before beginning this drill, coaches should emphasize visual fine centering on the offensive player's stomach. The offensive player begins at any one of the primary offensive areas (point, wing, corner)

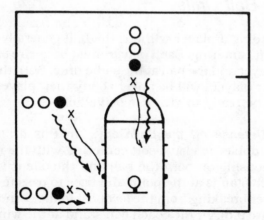

Figure 9.3 Drill 3—Defense Before the Dribble.

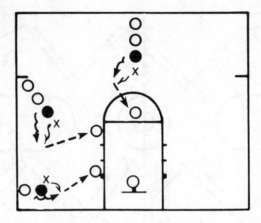

Figure 9.4 Drill 4—Defense After the Dribble.

and works one-on-one against the defender using crossover-step fakes or rocker-step fakes before dribbling. The defender must learn to ignore the head, foot, and ball fakes and to react only to the offensive player's stomach. Examples are shown in Figure 9.3.

Drill 4—Defense After the Dribble. This drill, illustrated in Figure 9.4, begins the same way as Drill 3 except the offensive player is allowed only one or two dribbles. When the offensive player picks up the ball, the defender must be there and defend against a pass to another offensive player.

Off-the-Ball Drills

Guarding a player without the ball generally requires visual soft centering. Each player must be aware of both his or her player and the ball at the same time. With this awareness your players will be able to deny their player the ball and will be ready to give defensive help.

Drill 5—Defense off the Ball/Deny. In this drill coaches should emphasize visual soft centering with the defensive player focusing on both the ball and the offensive player. The coach stands at the point and tries to pass to an offensive player breaking from the low post to the corner or wing (see Figure 9.5). Or the coach can stand at the wing and attempt to pass to the player breaking from the low post to

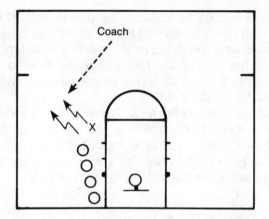

Figure 9.5 Drill 5—Defense off the Ball/Deny.

the corner or point. The defender's task is to see both the ball and the offensive player. If the defensive player is doing this, he or she should be able to intercept the coach's pass. When the pass is made the defensive player must shift his or her attention from soft centering on both the ball and the offensive player to fine centering on the ball only so that he or she may deflect or intercept the pass.

Drill 6—Defense off the Ball/Help. In this drill coaches should again emphasize visual soft centering on the ball and on the player. Two offensive and defensive players square

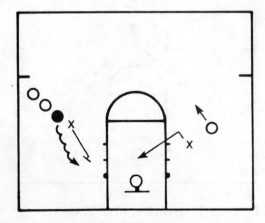

Figure 9.6 Drill 6—Defense off the Ball/Help.

off. The drill begins by having the player with the ball at one wing and the offensive player without the ball starting at a weakside position (wing or low post). The defender must deny his or her player the ball but move over to help out if the player with the ball drives to the basket. The pattern is illustrated in Figure 9.6.

In addition to performing these drills on the court, players also benefit from doing the visual control drills described in chapter 4, "Developing the Master Sense." These drills help to develop the visual soft centering skill that is necessary for providing defensive help.

Hearing and Touch Drills

You should also incorporate into your practice sessions defensive drills emphasizing talking, listening, and touch. These drills primarily involve the defender working to avoid a screen or fighting through a pick. The player fighting through the pick must listen to his or her teammate who is calling out the pick, "Pick right!" or "Pick left!" You should also designate some half-court scrimmages for the specific purpose of encouraging talking on defense. One drill you may use is shown in Figure 9.7. In this drill, Drill 7, the player guarding the ball must be centered in his or her visual system but must also be alert to teammates calling "pick

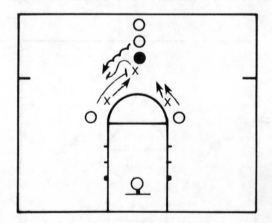

Figure 9.7 Drill 7—Hearing and Touch.

left" or "pick right." As the two offensive players attempt a pick-and-roll, the player guarding the ball must feel for the pick and fight through it.

Summary

Good defense begins by having the proper attitude. First, you must realize the importance of defense. There is more to basketball than scoring. Good teams and star players believe in giving their best offensively *and* defensively. Second, good defense requires an aggressive attitude and a willingness to take the initiative and force the offense into making mistakes. Third, good defense means being ready to act even when your player does not have the ball. You must be ready not only to deny your player the ball but also to assist teammates when the player with the ball becomes more dangerous than your player.

Good defense is also the result of proper concentration. Your focus of attention on defense is primarily visual and varies according to the situation. The proper visual awareness on defense depends on whether you are playing off the ball, guarding a player who has not yet used the dribble, guarding the dribbler, or guarding a player after the dribble. By developing the right attitude toward defense and developing proper practice and game concentration habits, anyone can become a sound defensive player.

Questions for Review

1. Why is attitude such an important part of defense?
2. Why is taking the initiative important on defense?
3. Why must you defend your player before he or she gets the ball?
4. Where should you be centering when your player has the ball and has not used his or her dribble?
5. Where should you be centering when your player is dribbling?
6. Where should you be centering when your player has picked up his or her dribble?

7. Why are anticipation and visualization important on defense?
8. Why is it important to talk on defense?
9. How can you use your sense of touch to your advantage on defense?
10. Why is flexibility of attention important on defense?
11. Why is knowledge of your opponent helpful on defense?

chapter 10

Rebounding Fundamentals

Basketball is basically a game of geometry—of lines, points and distances—and the horizontal distances are more important than the vertical ones. If I were playing against someone a foot shorter, the vertical distances could be important, but in competitive basketball, most of the critical distances are horizontal, along the floor or at eye level. Height is not as important as it may seem, even in rebounding. Early in my career at USF, watching rebounds closely, I was surprised to discover that three quarters of them were grabbed at or below the level of the basket—a height all college players can reach easily. (This is also true in the pro game.) Generally, the determining distances in those rebounds were horizontal ones.
—Bill Russell (Russell & Branch, 1979, p. 83)

Control of the boards is crucial to the outcome of every contest. Because an offensive rebound yields approximately one point per rebound for the offensive team, you must minimize your opponent's offensive rebounds while maximizing your own. The one rebound you do not pursue may be the difference between victory and defeat, so you must develop the habit of fighting for every rebound. No one can turn good habits on and off like a light. *Go for every rebound!*

To have a fair chance at each rebound, you should know the probable rebounding angle of the ball. This depends on the spot from which the shot is taken and on where it appears it will hit the board or basket. Knowing the probable rebounding distance is also important. Generally, three fourths of all rebounds come off the rim to the opposite side of the floor from where the shot was taken. The usual distance is about 3 to 4 feet from the basket.

Being a great rebounder takes persistence, persever-
ance, and an overwhelming desire to get the basketball. You
should never stand still and should spend every second
fighting for position. It's an all-out battle. On an intensity
scale of 1 to 10, with 1 being complete relaxation and 10
being maximum intensity, your rebounding intensity level
should be a "9." But battling at this level of intensity under
the boards takes its toll. To be able to maintain your concentration and high level of energy, you must be in tremendous condition. If you are in great condition, you will be able
to dominate the boards in the fourth quarter when your
opponent is tired and when it counts the most.

Two Tasks

In rebounding, you have two essential tasks—retrieving
the ball off the boards and preventing your opponent from
doing the same. Both tasks are made easier by having inside position on your opponent. Of course, the physical
qualities of size, strength, and leaping ability are important
factors. However, just as important are the mental factors
of attitude and concentration. These factors are the keys to
quickness, and *quickness* is the key to gaining inside position on your opponent. Quickness in gaining position is as
much mental as physical. Quick reaction as well as quick
action is important. Getting the jump is largely a result of

being alert, soft centering your vision on the court action, and reacting instantly to a shot attempt.

To get the jump on your opponent under the boards, you must assume two things:

1. Every shot will be missed and require a rebound effort in your area. *Don't wait to see if the shot is missed.*
2. Your opponent will try to rebound the missed shot.

These two assumptions require you to focus your attention on two things at once—your player and the ball.

Defensive Rebounding

Although no one denies the importance of rebounding, some people disagree on the best way to acquire the ball off the boards. Generally speaking, there are two primary theories on defensive rebounding. One theory stresses blocking each offensive player off the boards by making contact with the offensive player and then going after the ball. The second stresses playing the ball rather than the player. Both systems require that both objectives be met. The only difference is which goal receives more emphasis.

Method 1: Blocking Out

The basic goal of blocking out is to keep your opponent from getting the rebound. For this system to be effective, every player must concentrate on the player he or she is assigned to defend. If one player fails, the system breaks down. Therefore, each player needs to concentrate on the assigned opponent rather than on the ball.

To block out effectively and to maintain your advantageous position, you must step into your opponent, pivot, and hold off your player. This means you must focus your *vision* (visual fine centering) on your player as soon as a shot is taken. *Don't wait for the ball to bounce off the rim.* Block out your player as soon as the ball is in the air. As you pivot into your player, you must change your focus of attention to *touch*. By concentrating on your player through touch, you should be able to "read" his or her movements and move with that player, maintaining your floor advantage. However, at the same time, you must be visually alert even though you are not concentrating on the ball. If the ball comes into your area you must change your focus of attention, visually fine center on the ball, and go for it! Because you were not following the flight of the ball from the shooter's hand to the rim, you will reach the ball more slowly than if you just played the ball. However, if you concentrated on blocking out your player, you will have stopped him or her from securing the rebound.

In short, as a shot is taken you must immediately turn and step into your opponent, focusing all of your attention (all visual) on him or her. As you pivot, maintain position on your opponent by focusing two thirds of your attention on him or her (by touch), and relocate the ball by focusing one third of your attention on the ball (visual soft centering). If the ball is in your area, center your attention completely on the ball and go for it!

Method 2: Playing the Ball

Some coaches, like John Wooden, believe in having defensive rebounders play the ball rather than the opponent. In this system, as players turn to face the basket after a shot is attempted, they cross over into the path of their opponent and then *go for the ball.*

With this strategy, you must visually soft center your attention, keeping half your attention on the ball and half on your opponent for the split second you step in front of him or her. Once you step in front of your opponent, you must fine center your vision on the ball and judge its bounce off the rim so that you can grab the rebound at the height of your jump. This system is based on quickness to the ball—*he who hesitates is lost!*

Offensive Rebounding

When rebounding at the offensive end you must try to outmaneuver the defensive player while visually centering on the ball. If possible, avoid contact with the defender because most defenders maintain position by touch. Make him or her concentrate on finding you while you go for the ball.

Know the Shooter

Try to know *who* is shooting. Moses Malone, generally regarded as one of the game's best offensive rebounders, uses a system based on his knowledge of his teammates' shots. For his teammates who have soft, high, arching shots, he moves to the opposite side of the basket from where the shot is taken because the higher percentage of rebounds comes off there. For his teammates with low, flat shots, he moves to the side of the basket from where the shot is taken because a missed flat shot usually bounces off the front of the rim toward the shooter (White, February 3, 1979). Study your teammates' shots and program yourself accordingly.

Moses

Perhaps the best way to summarize the secret of great rebounding is to look at one of the best rebounders in the game today. Dwight Jones, once the backup center for Moses Malone at Houston, had this to say about the star player:

> *I think I've learned the secret of why [Moses] has become such a great rebounder. He's great because he's so intent at keeping his eye on the ball. You can push him, shove him, whack him, anything, but you can't make him take his eye off the ball. He's a classic picture of concentration. (White, 1979, p. 3)*

Coaches' Corner

The rebounding drills that you use in practice depend largely on your preference for blocking out or playing the ball. The drills listed here are classified as either blocking-out or playing-the-ball drills.

Blocking-Out Drills

If you prefer the blocking-out method, you must begin by drilling your players in the proper mechanics of a block-out. In this beginning stage players must learn to focus on body awareness until their step-and-pivot is automatic. Once players master the mechanics, they must perform drills requiring them to focus their attention on their player through touch. The next step is to put pairs of players (one offensive and one defensive) on the floor in a controlled scrimmage situation with an additional person (player or coach) taking shots from various spots on the floor. At this point players must be reminded to focus two thirds of their attention on their player through touch and one third of their attention on the ball. This stage should be played "live" with the offensive players making a real effort to get the ball.

Blocking Out—Mechanics Drill. Players line up on one sideline and are told to execute the step-and-pivot of the block-out. In this basic drill, players are instructed to focus on body awareness to master the mechanics more quickly.

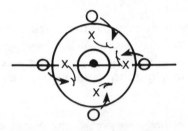

Figure 10.1 Blocking out—Center Circle Drill.

Blocking Out—Center Circle Drill. In this drill, illustrated in Figure 10.1, players learn to maintain their block-out inside position by focusing their attention on touch. The drill begins with four pairs of players setting up on the center circle equally spaced. A basketball is placed in the center of the circle. At the coach's command, the four inside players block out their partners and hold the block-out for 5 seconds or until one offensive player breaks through and grabs the ball. The outside players must try to fight around the block-out and get the ball. After each repetition, partners switch their inside and outside positions.

Blocking Out—Shell Drill. In this drill, five pairs of players set up at one basket in a "shell," with the five offensive players positioned on the outside and their partners set up

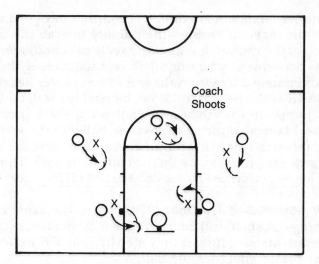

Figure 10.2   Blocking out—Shell Drill.

inside. When the coach shoots, the defensive five attempt to block out their partners while the offensive players fight for the rebound (see Figure 10.2). In this drill defensive players are reminded first to concentrate totally on their partner until the block-out is initiated, and then to focus two thirds of their attention on their player through touch and one third of their attention on the ball. Offensive and defensive players switch after each shot.

Playing-the-Ball Drills

If you prefer the playing-the-ball method, you probably want to spend some time doing rebounding "timing" drills before doing the controlled scrimmage drills. By timing drills I mean drills in which players pay close attention to the distance and arch of various shots and the resulting rebound angles and distance. In addition to learning the probable rebound area for various shots, players must practice timing their jump so that they grab the rebound at the height of their jump. In the controlled scrimmage or shell drill, you must emphasize the initial reaction of stepping in front of the offensive player before going for the ball. Because jumping is a crucial element of success in this strategy, conditioning drills for jumping should be performed regularly.

Off-the-Wall Rebounding Drill. This drill is designed to improve the players' timing—their ability to grab the ball at the top of their jump. It is also an excellent conditioner. The drill is performed by having all players stand along the gym approximately 3 feet from the wall. Each player has a ball. Players toss the ball 10 to 12 feet high off the wall and time their jumps so that they grab the ball at the top of their jumps. Players continue to toss the balls off the wall and "rip" rebounds for 2 or 3 minutes. A simple variation of the drill is to have the players tip the ball off the wall. This drill can also be performed by tossing the ball off the backboard.

Playing-the-Ball—Shell Drill. This drill is the same as the blocking-out shell drill except the defensive players do not block out; instead, they simply step in front of the offensive player before going for the ball.

Offensive Rebound Drills

Offensive rebounding drills can be performed at the same time as the controlled scrimmage drills for defensive rebounding. Offensive rebounders must be reminded to try to outmaneuver their defender to gain position or at least to distract the defender if he or she is trying to block out. The timing and conditioning drills described above are also good for developing offensive rebounders. Shooting drills in which one player rebounds while another player shoots have double value if the rebounders are asked to rip or tip the ball at the top of their jump.

Regardless of the method you prefer, you must have your players work at rebounding until it becomes second nature. Because so much of rebounding results from quickness, players cannot afford to pause and think. Instantaneous reaction is a must.

Summary

Defensive rebounding poses two opposing philosophies. One stresses playing the ball whereas the other stresses blocking out the opponent. Regardless of your defensive rebounding strategy, you must gain and maintain inside position. The same principle holds true for offensive rebounding. Secondly, although the physical qualities of size, strength, and leaping ability are important, the mental factors of attitude and concentration are just as important. These mental factors are the keys to quickness that in turn is the key to gaining inside position. The type of concentration required for rebounding varies, depending on whether you are on offense or on defense and whether you believe in blocking out or playing the ball. Finally, regardless of the method your team selects, you must work hard at rebounding until it becomes a habit.

Questions for Review

1. When a shot is taken, what two things must you assume to get the jump on your opponent?
2. Describe the type of concentration you need to block out on the boards.
3. Describe the proper concentration for playing the ball off the boards.
4. Where are most rebounds taken?
5. Where should you be moving to rebound a line drive shot?
6. Where should you be moving to rebound a high, arching shot?

chapter 11

Intensity

*Contrary to what you may have been told, hustle
does not nor cannot make up for lack of talent.
Hustle is an essential ingredient of talent, a good
deal more than the frantic energy of a banty rooster.
Hustle is the controlled perpetual motion of the
precision athlete. Hustle is John Havlicek.*
—Don Linehan (1976, p. 47)

Basketball is a game of constantly changing concentration and varying levels of intensity. Some aspects of the game, such as defense and rebounding, require almost maximum effort, whereas offense requires something less. For you to play your best, you not only must control your attention but also must exert the right level of energy for each situation that arises. This means that you must know what level of intensity is best for each situation and must be aware of your current intensity level so you can control it. You must be willing and able to put out maximum effort when necessary and must also be able to bring yourself down to a more relaxed state when you are too intense for a particular situation; for example, shooting.

An Intensity Scale

Perhaps the best way to illustrate the concept of optimum intensity is by creating an Intensity Scale as shown in Table 11.1. On this scale, "1" represents complete relaxation, such as a person sleeping or meditating. A "10" represents maximum intensity accompanied by mild symptoms of the fight-or-flight syndrome. At the "9.5" level is the player who is simply trying too hard. At the "9" level is the player going all out but not fighting him- or herself. An "8" is an 80% effort, and so forth.

According to this scale, a fine coordination skill like shooting requires a lower intensity level than playing defense. The reason for this is simple. When you shoot a basketball you must first flex your shooting arm by bending it at a 90° angle at the elbow. You do this by contracting your biceps (front upper arm muscles) and relaxing your triceps (back upper arm muscles). Once you have the ball in the "ready" position, you extend your arm up toward the basket by relaxing your biceps and contracting your triceps. If you are trying too hard or are emotionally overexcited and tense, you overcontract your triceps and don't relax your biceps. You create an inefficient movement pattern by

Table 11.1 The Intensity Scale

Rating	Description
10	Maximum effort accompanied by mild symptoms of the fight-or-flight syndrome
9.5	Trying too hard, out-of-control, but not necessarily too tense
9	Almost all-out effort, playing hard but not hypertense (rebounding, defensive pressure, getting back on "D")
8	80% effort or speed (inside power moves, cutting, defensive help)
7	70% effort or speed (receiving, shooting on the move, driving)
6	60% effort
5	50% effort
4	Little physical effort (free throws)
3	30% effort
2	20% effort
1	Complete relaxation (sleeping or meditating)

extending your arm out in front of you rather than upward. You also tend to pull your arm back after the ball is released rather than follow through. In this instance, your shot is flat with no backspin. When you try too hard or are too tense, you fight yourself; your opposing muscles lack the fine coordination necessary for performing fine motor skills like shooting, passing, and receiving. On the other hand, high intensity is productive in relatively uncomplicated skills like playing defense and rebounding. In these areas, strength and aggressiveness are much more important than fine muscle coordination. In short, your level of intensity varies according to the basketball skill you are performing.

Offensive Intensity

Offensive intensity varies with the task at hand. However, one general principle applies. Because of the ball-handling skill required on offense, whether it be passing, receiving, dribbling, or shooting, your intensity level must be significantly lower than when you are playing defense and under the boards. The fine coordination necessary for these skills makes relaxation a must. Operating on a "9" or "10" level of intensity impairs the control and follow-through necessary for executing the fundamentals. Generally, the levels of offensive intensity described in Table 11.2 are best:

Table 11.2 Effective Intensity Levels for Offensive Play

Rating	Description
9.5-10	As an offensive player you should *never* play at a "9.5" or "10" level of intensity. If you are too tense, practice the relaxation exercises discussed in chapter 17, "Coping With Competition: The ABCs."
9	Filling the fast break lanes and offensive rebounding
8	Making inside power moves, cutting without the ball
7	Receiving, shooting on the move, driving
4	Shooting free throws (use relaxation exercises before shooting)

Defensive Intensity

The offensive player has a significant advantage over the defensive player because the offensive player knows what he or she is going to do. The defensive player can only react to the offensive player's initiative. This advantage is partially counterbalanced by the fact that the offensive player operates best at a "7" level of intensity (or 70% speed) because of the sharp cuts and ball-handling skills required. Nevertheless, the offensive player has the advantage in a one-on-one situation.

To compensate for the disadvantage of needing to react to the offensive player's initiative, the defender must play the ball-handler at a "9" level of intensity. Even when guarding a ball-handler who is not looking to score, the defender must pressure the ball-handler at a "9" level of intensity to prevent him or her from seeing the court well. Defenders off the ball must be ready to help at an "8" level of intensity. This higher level of intensity on defense is appropriate because the defensive player does not execute the fine coordination skills of the offensive player; he or she does not need to be under the same control as the offensive player. In short, the defender must play at a "9" level of intensity to:

- make up for reacting to the offensive player's initiative and being one step behind;
- disrupt the offensive player's vision as much as possible; and
- force the offensive player to move at an "8" or "9" speed where he or she is less likely to operate with precision and more likely to make mistakes.

Rebounding Intensity

Rebounding requires more than mere height and strength; it takes tenacity, perseverence, and an overwhelming desire to get the basketball. You must never stand still. You should devote your energy to fighting for position. Your level of intensity under the boards should be just under the maximum intensity level because you are literally fighting for the ball. If you are not willing to expend the necessary energy, you are unlikely to get more than the few rebounds that fall into your lap.

Conditioning

Basketball is an exceptionally strenuous game because of its constant movement, sudden stops and starts, quick changes of direction and speed, jumping, defensive sliding, and bumping under the boards. *You must be in tremendous condition to bear the strain that the intensity of excellence requires.* You are lucky if you have a coach who drills you hard to get you into top shape. Most athletes cannot push themselves to that point. Those athletes who are in top condition can play at a "9" level of intensity when needed, whereas those not in good shape slip to a "7" or "8" level of intensity in the second half when the game is on the line. Remember, you can always use the relaxation exercises (discussed in chapter 17, "Coping With Competition: The ABCs") to lower yourself from an overaroused state during a game. But you can do nothing during a game to make up for fatigue and lack of energy. You must work hard in practice to gain the conditioning needed to play competitive basketball.

Coaches' Corner

Playing basketball at optimum intensity should be a mental and moral matter, not an emotional one. The coach who charges up his or her players emotionally before a game with inspiring pep talks is doing more harm than good. A "psyched up" player or team operates at an overexcited level, one or two steps above what is best. The extra tension or excitement usually results in poor shooting (no follow-through), turnovers (traveling, fumbled passes), and over-aggressive defense (hacking). Moreover, coaches who try to "move" their players rather than motivate them will soon find that spine-tingling speeches do not affect their players at all. Also, when coaches give their players an overly rousing pep talk for the big game, they will find their players unmotivated for the less important one. These coaches will not see playing intensity until it is too late. Their players will be playing at a level of intensity one step below what is needed, resulting in sluggish defense and sloppy offense.

Rather than working on his or her players' emotions, a coach must work on developing appropriate attitudes and habits. They do this by encouraging a commitment to excellence and the best performance possible, regardless of the situation. By forming positive habits, developing intensity awareness, and demanding proper intensity habits, the coach will have a team playing at optimum levels in practice and all games. Players must learn that they cannot turn emotional energy on and off like a light. They must be willing in practice to develop proper intensity habits based on attitude (a commitment to excellence) rather than on emotion.

In short, the teams that play on mental and moral plains rather than at emotional peaks and valleys will be able to consistently play hard and loose instead of high and tight on some days and low and lifeless on other days.

Summary

Basketball is best played at varying levels of intensity with the appropriate level depending on the situation and the task at hand. You must understand the best playing levels for each phase of the game—offense, defense, and rebounding—and must be willing to develop playing habits consistent with those intensity levels. *You* must be able to monitor your intensity level during a contest and to make adjustments when necessary.

Remember, too, that willpower alone is not enough to see you through a game at high levels of intensity. The physical demands of basketball require you to be in top condition. You must be in shape to maintain a high level of intensity throughout a contest and to free your mind from the distraction of fatigue. Concentration, composure, and confidence leave you in direct proportion to the onset of fatigue.

Questions for Review

1. Briefly describe the intensity scale.
2. What level of intensity should you be playing at for rebounding, playing pressure defense, and getting back on defense?

3. What level of intensity is best for making inside power moves, cutting, and helping on defense?
4. What level of intensity is best for receiving, shooting on the move, and driving?
5. What danger is there in a coach giving an inspiring pep talk before a game?
6. Why should intensity be based on attitude and habits rather than on emotion?

chapter 12

Quickness

> I have repeatedly pointed out that basketball is a
> mental game and quickness is probably the greatest
> physical asset a player can have. These qualities
> certainly go hand in hand as it takes mental alert-
> ness to put your quickness into action and at the
> proper time. . . . Quickness of thought and action,
> then, is a characteristic that stands out very
> prominently in the star performers. Basketball is a
> game of habits and reactions and the players who
> cannot react instantaneously to situations will be the
> second-raters because they will lose so many
> opportunities.
> —John Wooden (1966, p. 131)

Although basketball is a full-court game in which
players must sprint the length of the court many times, most
of the essential action occurs only after both teams are set
up offensively and defensively at one end of the court or the
other. At that time, you must either elude your opponent
on offense or stick with him or her on defense. To get open
on offense requires quick stops and starts, not a full-court
sprint. Basketball is a game primarily of two, three, or four
steps. Within those steps, the offensive player must earn a
one-step advantage to get open for a shot. Hence, *quickness*,
not speed, is the essential factor.

Quickness Is
More Mental Than Physical

Gaining the one-step advantage on your opponent is
more mental than physical! Strength, coordination, and

endurance are important, but visual awareness, reaction, and anticipation are even more important. These key factors exist in your mind, not your muscles.

Muscle Quickness

Strong, long legs propel you more quickly and farther in three steps than weak, stubby legs do. But on high levels of competition, players' physical differences are *not* that great. On the professional level they're almost negligible. Players have few differences in coordination and body mechanics as well, even at the high school level. Finally, endurance, which enables you to maintain your quickness at the end of the game, is a matter of conditioning. Because endurance is developed by working hard beyond the point of fatigue, it is more a matter of desire than strength.

Mental Quickness

Any physical movement results from a three-step process of the mind. Before you can make the correct move in a situation, your mind must have the information necessary to make a sound decision and to direct the body.

Awareness. The necessary information is acquired and sent to your mind through your body's senses (vision, hearing, touch, etc.). Because you receive information from all of your senses at the same time, you must learn to center your attention on the most important information. In basketball, this information is usually visual. For example, if your mind is focused on the important cues (the open player) rather than on some distraction (the crowd), you will be able to make the right play (a pass) *the instant* the play develops. On the other hand, if your mind is focused on a mental replay of the play you just muffed at the other end of the court (a distraction) or on feelings of fatigue (wrong cues), you will make a *slow* or even a wrong decision. The first principle of mental quickness is to *maintain your concentration on the most important cues.*

Quick Reaction. Once you are aware of the important cues in a situation, you must make an instant decision based on the facts. Should you shoot, drive, cut, pass, front your player, switch? You can make these decisions automatically only if they have been "preprogrammed." In other words, you must already know what you are going to do in a particular situation when that situation arises. Overlearning responses so you do them quickly and subconsciously through habit is essential for top performance.

The only way to overlearn a response is to perform the desired behavior repeatedly. You may do this either by going out on the court and actually performing the desired action in drills or by visualizing the action in mental rehearsal. Coaches can simplify the development of mental quickness by developing easy strategies and systems of play (the *KISS* theory—***Keep It Simple Stupid***), but only you, the athlete, can control how well you have overlearned the team's philosophy, systems of play, and strategy.

Anticipation. Anticipation is the art of visualizing a situation or play and your reaction to it, before it actually happens. Anticipation is very advantageous because it quickens your response and puts you one step ahead of your opponent. This mental, one-step advantage is achieved only through the combination of proper visual awareness and visualization.

Even though anticipation can be dangerous (it can backfire on you if you're wrong), it is a necessary risk that you must take to have a one-step advantage on offense or to make up a one-step disadvantage on defense. You can lessen the risks, however, by knowing your teammates' court habits and your opponents' strategy and habits. Being a student of the game pays off handsomely by enabling you to be mentally quick.

Balance

Before summarizing this chapter, a short note is required on the relationship between balance and quickness, especially in regard to the "big man." Part of the reason posts or centers are often slower than guards is that in many cases, the taller players have not developed their sense of balance to the degree that they are willing to go all out on the court. They tend to hold back to maintain body control. This is unfortunate because body balance is easy to develop.

For players who especially need to develop balance and coordination, I recommend the balance beam and trampoline drills described in chapter 15, "Mind Games."

Summary

Basketball is a game of quickness. To get open for a shot on offense or to receive the ball in an advantageous position, you must be quick enough to gain at least a one-step advantage on your defender. On defense quickness helps prevent your opponent from getting a step on you. Quickness is more mental than physical because the necessary one-step advantage is usually created on the first step. That crucial first step is gained by having proper awareness, reacting instantaneously, and anticipating well.

Questions for Review

1. Why is quickness so important in basketball?
2. Why is getting the one-step advantage more mental than physical?
3. What is the key to mental quickness?
4. What is the key to quick reaction?
5. Why is anticipation so important?

part 3

Halftime

The Mind in Athletics and Strength Training

Weight lifting is all "mind over matter." As long as the mind can envision the fact that you can do something, you can. . . . I visualized myself being there already—having achieved the goal already. Working out is just the physical follow-through, a reminder of the vision you're focusing on.
—Arnold Schwarzennegger (Ostrander & Schroeder, 1979, p. 147)

SCENE: WNBA-TV studio in New York where host Mike Rofone is about to interview Jay Mikes during halftime of the Saturday afternoon game of the week.

MIKE: Good afternoon. I'm Mike Rofone and it's time for another halftime special feature. Today we're going to talk about an aspect of basketball training that has become increasingly popular among coaches and players—weight training. But before you get up and head to the refrigerator saying to yourself, "I know all about that," let me tell you, if you think weight training is only about bench pressing, arm curls, and muscles, you're in for a real treat today.

Today we'll be talking to Jay Mikes, author of *Basketball Fundamentals*. Jay will discuss the *mental* aspects of athletics and strength training. Good afternoon, Coach.

JAY: Good afternoon. It's a pleasure to be here.

MIKE: First, Jay, tell us, why is strength training important in basketball? I know some coaches, John Wooden for example, are opposed to weight training for their athletes. Why do you think it is important?

JAY: Strength training is important for two reasons, Mike. First, research indicates that strength training improves power and quickness without sacrificing skill. The old idea was that if athletes strength trained, they would become muscle-bound and lose their flexibility and their skills would diminish. Now we know that isn't true. Second, as a player becomes stronger through training, his or her self-image changes. The player becomes more confident of holding his or her own in a physical sense. As a result, the athlete becomes more aggressive under the boards and on defense.

MIKE: I'll buy that. But tell us, how important is the mind when it comes to weight lifting and body-building? Is the mind really that important?

JAY: Mike, the progress of every athlete, whether a bodybuilder or a basketball player, totally depends on the athlete's use of the mind. Most people are unaware of the mind's functions and therefore lack the ability to use their training to their best advantage.

MIKE: Can you be specific and give us some insight on how the mind works?

JAY: Sure. To put it simply, the human mind works on two levels—the conscious and the subconscious. The *conscious mind* simply refers to those thoughts of which we are aware, what we are thinking at the moment. The *subconscious* mind, on the other hand, refers to the mental processes constantly in operation that we do not sense but that control most of our mental and physical processes. Let me explain.

MIKE: Please do.

JAY: There are four types of conscious thought. The first type is pure *sensory awareness*. Sensory awareness is simply focusing your conscious attention on the sensations of any one of your sensory systems, such as vision, hearing, touch, taste, smell, and body awareness. All of our early learning in life comes from sensory awareness.

As we experience the countless number of sensory impressions, our minds begin to organize them in patterns and store them away in our subconscious memory banks. These impressions are later recalled through the developing power of *imagination*, or the ability to bring to mind images or impressions of past sensory experiences. Imagination is the second type of conscious thought.

The third type of conscious thought that is distinctly human in nature is *verbalization*. It is the "inner voice" of our minds.

The fourth type of conscious thought is *mind awareness*, which is simply awareness of our conscious awareness.

MIKE: How is the conscious mind used in athletics?

JAY: The conscious mind has two basic purposes in athletics. The first is to provide us with awareness of the competitive situation, which I'll discuss in a moment. The second is to select goals. Through the power of imagination, the conscious mind selects our goals, beginning a process of channeling our energies toward goal attainment.

MIKE: How does the subconscious mind fit in?

JAY: The best way I can explain it is to compare the subconscious to a computer. The subconscious has two major parts. The first part functions like a computer *data disk* and stores all our experiences, including all the perceptions taken in by our senses and our conclusions and judgments about those things we perceive. This includes all our sensory impressions acquired on the basketball court and the judgments we make about these impressions such as, "I'm a poor shooter" or "I'm a great defensive player." The data disk is constantly being updated as our experiences grow and our conclusions change. The impact of the data disk on your performance is critical and I'll explain that in detail in a moment.

The second major part of the subconscious mind is the *program disk*. The program disk provides mental methods for accomplishing goals. It is responsible for all overlearned skills such as walking, writing, chewing, dribbling, or shooting.

The programs for these various skills are formulated through experience by trial and error. The program disk relies heavily on the information in the data disk. What we normally call thinking is the interaction between these disks.

MIKE: I see. But how do the two minds interact in athletics?

JAY: Using the computer analogy again, the athlete's thought processes involve three phases—input, processing, and output. We'll simply refer to these phases as *awareness* (input), *thinking* (processing), and *directing* (output).

An athlete must first have the proper input to make the right play in a given situation. This is where the conscious mind plays a role. The sensory systems of vision, hearing, touch, body awareness, and balance give the athlete the information to feed into the computer mind. As a general rule, if the input is poor, the output or performance is not much better.

MIKE: That's why concentration is so important in athletics.

JAY: Precisely.

MIKE: What happens after the input has been received?

JAY: Once an athlete has acquired the important information, his or her mind can interpret and analyze the situation based on experiences stored in his or her data disk. The experienced player, with a wealth of data at his or her disposal, knows the best response to a particular situation, making the processing phase automatic. An experienced player does not need to think consciously through a response. In fact, conscious thinking is a handicap because conscious thought takes time, a luxury not often available to an athlete.

For example, the ball-handler on a three-on-two fast break dribbles the ball to the free throw line and is stopped by one defender. The ball-handler sees that his or her teammate on the left is guarded, whereas the other teammate on the right is open and cutting to the basket. The ball-handler's decision to pass the ball to the teammate on the right, along with the judgment on where to pass the ball to reach the player in stride, is best accomplished when there is no conscious thinking. Magic Johnson describes this phenomenon correctly when he says, "It just happens . . . pow!" (Newman, 1984, p. 15). This is thinking that occurs below the conscious level.

MIKE: So you're saying the first phase, *awareness*, occurs on the conscious level but the second phase, *processing* or *thinking*, occurs on the subconscious level. Is that right?

JAY: Yes.

MIKE: From what you're saying, then, the subconscious is pretty important in athletics.

JAY: Exactly. But that's not all. When a physical movement has been decided, the program disk sends out electrical impulses through the nervous system to the body parts, directing the contraction of the muscles and the expenditure of energy that produces movement and maintains the body's balance. The athlete does not consciously think about moving each body part in sequence. The program disk does this on the subconscious level. The athlete's performance depends largely on the program that has been established in the subconscious.

MIKE: At this point I am led to believe that in athletics, the subconscious is more important than the conscious mind. Is this true?

JAY: Well, there's more. Not only does the subconscious mind control the body, *it also controls the conscious mind*, causing it to focus on one of the four conscious thought processes. In other words, the subconscious mind directs the athlete's concentration. Again, the best results are achieved through established concentration programs or habits, and in this case the habits are mental, not physical.

MIKE: That is interesting. I never realized the subconscious is so important.

JAY: It is, Mike. And for the sake of our viewers, I have brought in a diagram (see Figure 13.1) that should make understanding the mind in athletics as simple as shooting a lay-up. Keep in mind, however, that this diagram is not meant to represent the actual locations of the conscious and subconscious mind in the brain itself. The diagram is merely a representation of the athlete's mental processes.

MIKE: Let me ask you something. As a kid, I dreamed of becoming a professional athlete. I used my conscious mind when dreaming of the "ultimate" goal. What happened? Was there something wrong with my subconscious?

JAY: No, Mike. There was nothing wrong with your subconscious, only the way you programmed it.

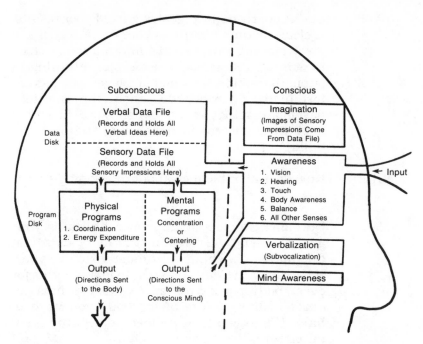

Figure 13.1 Subconscious and conscious mental processes.

There are other factors, too, that may have denied you your dream, such as the type of training you received or the physical tools you had.

MIKE: In a way, it appears that the conscious mind has little to do with athletic achievement.

JAY: In a way you're right. But again, the process begins by selecting clear goals and channeling all your energy into the achievement of those goals. Selecting goals and developing a clear image of your goals through the use of your imagination are the products of the conscious mind.

MIKE: So you're saying a basketball player who wants to improve his or her game must begin by using the conscious mind to choose and define his or her goal.

JAY: Yes. A poorly defined goal will yield poor results. A clear, distinct *picture* of your desired goal will give your subconscious the information it needs to achieve the goal. For example, returning to strength training, a basketball player who has not formulated an exact idea about the muscular development that he or she wishes to achieve will have little success in developing strength and bulk.

MIKE: How does an athlete go about developing a clear goal?

JAY: Developing a clear goal involves affirming your goal over and over again. It is more than just dreaming or wishing. You must visualize yourself exactly the way you want to look. Do this for every body part. Work at it until you have an exact mental picture of the body you want to have. When you have defined your entire mental picture, think about it often.

MIKE: What does it take for an athlete to achieve a goal?

JAY: Achieving your goal depends on how realistic your goal is, how far you are from your goal, and how much motivation you have to pursue it. Setting goals and believing in their achievement are, therefore, your most important tasks. You must focus your mind on your goal and think of it often to reinforce the goal in your subconscious mind.

MIKE: In other words, what you think is what you get.

JAY: That's right, if it is within your physical potential and your control.

MIKE: Well, obviously setting goals is very important. But that happens before you lie down on the bench. Can you tell us what should be going through your mind when you're actually performing weight-training exercises?

JAY: The state of mind you must have when performing a set of any exercise is called *concentration twilight*—the physical and mental interaction of mind and body (Ross, 1978).

MIKE: Can you describe this state of mind?

JAY: *Concentration twilight* is a state of mind in which intense body awareness intermingles with the magic of imagination. Each repetition takes you to a new world of images. The only boundaries of this new dimension are the images themselves and a signpost ahead reading, *"WARNING! FATIGUE, DISCOMFORT, AND NAUSEA AHEAD!"*

As the discomfort increases with each repetition, the images grow more vivid. In your mind you see scenes from past NBA play-off wars. You see Daryl Dawkins rising above the crowd with his arm cocked, muscles flexed, poised and ready to tear the rim off with a powerful, backboard-shattering slam dunk. More reps . . . and the image you have is not Daryl Dawkins—it's you! Then more reps. Discipline lets you forget the discomfort, the fatigue, and even the nausea. It enables you to rivet your mind on the image of the goal you wish to attain. This discipline, the state of concentration twilight, enables you to overcome the discomfort barrier with violent determination. It lifts you into an unknown area of force, beyond your usual effort by concentrating on vivid images of your goal.

MIKE: By discomfort, do you also mean pain? Should an athlete keep pushing beyond the point of pain?

JAY: Absolutely not! Athletes must acknowledge that pain is telling them something. Pain signals an injury. So you shouldn't ignore pain. You must stop to prevent a more serious injury. Push yourself beyond the point of discomfort but not beyond the point of pain.

MIKE: Is concentration twilight a state of mind anyone can develop?

JAY: Learning the state of concentration twilight takes only a short time for the beginner to achieve.

Once concentration twilight is mastered, the discomfort and fatigue becomes a sign post saying *"PUSH YOURSELF FURTHER!"* To go further is to win a personal battle with the person who gives you your stiffest competition—you. Can you beat this person? If you want to—that is, if you have the guts—you will ignore the fatigue, discomfort, and nausea and forge ahead, not occasionally, but in every training session.

MIKE: What happens if you lose your concentration?

JAY: If at some moment you lose concentration before the point of discomfort, recover it, or your set will go for nothing. Bodybuilders who are not paying attention to their physical and mental impressions benefit relatively little from their workouts.

MIKE: Well, you've made me a believer in "mind over matter." But how far can an athlete go? Are there limits? One problem that confronts most weight lifters is the so-called "sticking point," the plateau where the athlete seems to have reached his or her limit. How do you go beyond it?

JAY: Maybe I can answer that by relating a true story. For a long time, 500 pounds had been an impenetrable barrier for weight lifters, just as the 4-minute mile had once been a barrier for runners. Then Vasily Alexeyev, the great Russian weight lifter, had an interesting experience on his way to the gold medal in the 1976 Olympics. Alexeyev and others lifted bars just below the 500-pound cut-off point. In one event, his trainers told him that he was about to lift his world record: 499.9 pounds. He did. Then they weighed the bar and showed him it was actually 501½ pounds. A few years later at the Olympics, Alexeyev raised 564 pounds.

MIKE: That's incredible. Or maybe it isn't. Maybe we're just beginning to discover our potential as human beings. The role of the mind in athletics is such a fascinating subject.

Unfortunately, we're out of time. Thank you for joining us. See you next week.

Questions for Review

1. What is the purpose of the the conscious mind?
2. What is the purpose of the subconscious?
3. What is the data disk?
4. What is the program disk? Why is the development of habits important in basketball?
5. Why is the selection of goals important?
6. Describe the state of concentration twilight.

part 4

Third Quarter: Mental Practice

chapter 14

Suggestology and Mental Rehearsal: Easy-Chair Drills

Whenever the dialogue stops, the world collapses and extraordinary facets of ourselves surface, as though they had been kept heavily guarded by our words. You are like you are, because you tell yourself that you are that way.
—Carlos Castaneda (1974, p. 40)

Your attention can focus on one of four things—*sensations* of any one of your senses, *images* of the past or future, *verbal messages* from your own inner voice, or *reflections* on the mind itself (mind awareness). So far this book has dealt primarily with the first of these thought processes and has shown how your awareness of the present influences your performance on the court. However, concentration is not the only "mental stuff" of sports during a contest. Your subconscious thoughts and feelings also affect your performance. In this chapter you will learn how to use your other mental processes of imagination and subverbalization (inner voice) to unlock the powers of your subconscious and to overcome the negative thoughts that limit your potential. You will explore two mental training methods that you can do in bed or in your favorite easy chair. These training methods can and will help you reach your potential.

Who Uses Mental Rehearsal?

Every athlete uses suggestology and mental rehearsal to some degree. This is because the instructions from your mind to your body are in the form of subverbalization (unspoken words) or imagination (thinking in pictures or images). Singer (1972) tells us that talking to ourselves is a useful learning device that helps us to acquire skills. Most outstanding athletes practice some form of verbalization in developing their skills.

Although you use your subverbal thought processes in learning skills, your actual use of subverbalization *during* performance is limited. Research shows that during competition, athletes think in terms of *images* rather than words (Nideffer, 1976). If you spend a good deal of time on the court paying attention to what you are saying to yourself, you destroy your concentration and ruin your composure and confidence as well. Usually, players talk to themselves the most when things are going wrong, with comments like: "Oh, man! Give me a break!"; "I can't hit anything tonight!"; or "If that jerk pushes me one more time he's gonna get an elbow in his gut!"

Any time subvocalization is negative, it disrupts your composure and confidence. Any time subvocalization occurs while the clock is running, it breaks your concentration. Again, this is because you cannot focus your attention on your internal dialogue and on sensory information at the same time. Even if your subverbalization is positive, you may still draw your attention away from where it should be. During competition you must keep your eye (and mind) on the game, not on your internal dialogue.

In short, you cannot learn to do anything athletic without using your mental processes of subverbalization and imagination. During competition, however, you must focus primarily on your vision and body awareness and not on your inner voice. The difference between successful and unsuccessful athletes stems largely from differences in their use of verbalization, imagination, and concentration. Everyone uses these three mind processes. What counts is *how* and *when* you use them.

Mental Training in America

American athletes are just beginning to use mind development programs. Our foreign competitors are much more advanced than us in this regard. The Russians have experimented with mental training in athletics since the 1940s. The East Germans have also long used mental training in their national sport-training programs. According to Ostrander and Schroeder (1979), psychological training is probably one reason that the Russians and East Germans have performed so well in the Olympics.

In the United States, primarily gymnasts, swimmers, divers, and skaters have used mental rehearsal. Recently, however, football, baseball, and basketball players have also begun psychological training. For example, the University of Illinois football and basketball teams, 1983-84 Big Ten Champions, employ mental training techniques. In his book, *Second Wind* (Russell & Branch, 1979), Bill Russell describes his discovery of the power of imagination that transformed him from a mediocre high school player into a collegiate All-American.

The growing use of mental rehearsal and suggestology techniques can be attributed to the influx of mental training books in the last decade. Many are listed in the references at the end of this book, and new ones are released each year. The next few sections describe the developing art and science of mental rehearsal and suggestology.

Mental Rehearsal

Mental rehearsal is the use of imagination to bring to mind reproductions of the sensations and feelings experienced in performing a skill. Its purpose is to improve skills, coordination, confidence, composure, and concentration. However, mental rehearsal is more than simple daydreaming. The athlete does more than watch a mental movie of him- or herself in action. Rehearsal, as opposed to simple imagery, involves actively studying an image or a series of images. One can develop an image of a movement without necessarily analyzing its content. Mental rehearsal also involves more than just visual imagery; it involves using *all* the body's senses, if possible, to *feel* as well as see an act. Vivid mental rehearsal re-creates in the athlete's mind the roar of the crowd (sound), the color of the uniforms (sight), the texture of the ball (feel), the rhythm of movement (body awareness), and the agony of pain and fatigue (body awareness).

Suggestology

Just as mental rehearsal uses the power of imagination to develop physical and mental skills and attributes, *suggestology* uses subverbalization (thinking in words) to improve concentration, confidence, composure, and self-concept. In suggestology, you repeat positive instructions subvocally to yourself while reclining in bed or sitting in an easy chair. You begin by repeating short phrases to relax your body and to clear your mind. After reaching a state of relaxation, you mentally recite phrases to yourself that build your self-image, improve your concentration, and refine your technique.

Mental Training and Self-Image

One of the greatest limitations on any athlete is his or her own self-image. An athlete with a poor self-image and a negative attitude will perform poorly. In Stan Kellner's classic, *Taking It to the Limit*, the author explains four basic laws of the mind:

1. *The self-image determines performance.*
2. *Improve the self-image and performance improves.*
3. *The mind does not always know the difference between a real and an imagined experience.*
4. *Each player has a success mechanism—the subconscious mind. (1978, p. 17)*

In other words, every athlete performs on the court according to the self-image "videotapes" stored in his or her subconscious. If the athlete's performance videotapes are negative (shooting bricks, dropping passes, fouling clumsily, reacting slowly) as a result of poor past performances, his or her present performance is likely to suffer. The past dictates the present because the body simply acts out the directions that the subconscious mind gives it (in this case, negative images of playing potential). In short, improved performance begins with an improved self-image.

Negative Subvocalization

What you think of yourself or your performance is formed largely by what you tell yourself before, during, and after a contest. Rather than use the power of positive suggestion to increase concentration, confidence, composure, and intensity, you bombard your self-concept with negative thoughts. These negative self-statements destroy concentration, erode confidence, create anxiety, increase muscle tension, and produce tentative play. To play to your potential you must overcome the habit of negative subvocalization that limits your performance.

"Relative," Negative Thinking

An athlete's self-image that is "relatively" poor can also negatively affect performance. For example, a Division I All-Conference college player can have a very positive self-image when playing in conference games. However, the same player, when trying out for the U.S. Olympic team against other All-Conference and All-American players, might have a relatively negative self-image. This athlete knows he or she is a good player but is not sure if he or she is "as good" as the other star players. On this higher level of competition, the athlete's confidence becomes shaky. This uncertainty or lack of confidence often causes very good athletes to play below their potential. The "relative" lack of confidence affects the athlete's composure and in turn affects concentration and execution. In other words, even a top player can be affected by a negative self-image.

The Value of Mental Training in Improving Self-Image

The value of mental rehearsal and suggestology is their ability to change an athlete's negative self-image into a positive one. An athlete who has had little success and therefore has a negative self-image can create successful experiences and a positive self-image through the powers of imagination and subverbalization. The "magic" behind mental rehearsal and suggestology is the fact that the mind does not always differentiate between a *real* experience and a vividly *imagined* experience.

An Exercise in Imagery. To prove this principle to yourself, try this mental exercise:

> *Close your eyes. Imagine that you are holding a lemon. It is in your right hand. You can feel the coolness and waxy texture of its yellow skin. Try squeezing it a little. Can you feel its firmness? Smell the lemon. Now, mentally cut the lemon with a knife, bite deeply into it and taste its tart and sour flavor. If you have used your imagination, by this time your mouth is watering. (Kellner, 1978, p. 36)*

The Famous Free Throw Experiment. Despite the effectiveness of the lemon demonstration, you may be saying to yourself, "What does drooling over the image of a lemon have to do with improving basketball skill?" The answer lies in a famous experiment. In a study of the effect of mental rehearsal on athletic performance, a class of college students was divided into three groups. None of the students were basketball players. At the beginning of the experiment, all students were tested and scored on their ability to shoot free throws. During the next 20 days, Group 1 was required to practice 20 minutes a day. Group 2 was the control group and did not practice at all. Group 3 was required to shoot *imaginary* free throws for 20 minutes a day; that is, they used mental imagery to develop skill. They were not allowed to do any real practice. At the end of the experiment all students were tested again. The results were amazing. The control group that did not practice performed the same as they did on the first test and showed no improvement. Group 1, which actually shot practice free throws for 20 minutes a day, improved 24%. Group 3, which used mental rehearsal only, improved 23%! In other words, the students who used mental imagery techniques improved almost as much as those who actually practiced free throws (Clark, 1960). Remember, physical practice *is* necessary. But it is a good idea to supplement your physical practice with mental practice.

Although the effectiveness of mental rehearsal is astounding, the best news is that your imagined experiences can always be successful. These successful experiences can turn your negative self-image into a positive one. Positive mental rehearsal and suggestology can be used in many ways to work on specific skills, moves, techniques, concentration, composure, or intensity—all while relaxing comfortably in your favorite easy chair.

Using Suggestology and Mental Rehearsal

Suggestology and mental rehearsal can be used almost anytime, anywhere. You can use them before a game to prepare for competition. You can use them during a game at breaks in the action to reinforce a positive frame of mind or after a game to learn from competition. You can use them at home before and after practice to reinforce learning or in the off-season to accelerate your development. But perhaps the best time to use suggestology and mental rehearsal is before you fall asleep in bed. At that time your subconscious is most susceptible to the powers of imagination and suggestion.

How to Practice

Mental rehearsal and suggestology exercises are simple to perform. Each one involves a four-step process with the fourth step being the only difference between the two methods. Step 4 in mental rehearsal utilizes the *power of imagination*. Step 4 in suggestology utilizes the *power of suggestion*.

Step 1: Choose a Goal. The first step in either technique is to choose a goal. Do you want to improve a particular skill? Do you want sharper, more flexible concentration? Do you want greater composure on the court? Do you want to build your confidence and self-image? The choice is yours. It can be based on your own self-analysis or on your coach's recommendation. The important factor is that you have a clear, realistic, yet challenging performance goal in mind before beginning your easy-chair drills.

Step 2: Find a Quiet Place.   The second step is to find a quiet place, free from distractions. It can be your own bed where you can lie comfortably, or it can be your favorite easy chair. It doesn't matter which you choose, as long as you know you can relax there undisturbed for 20 or 30 minutes.

Step 3: Relaxation.   After you are situated, the next step is to perform a short series of isometric contractions, tensing and relaxing your muscles from head to toe to relax your body. Then close your eyes and perform a simple deep-breathing exercise. Slowly, to the count of four (one thousand one, one thousand two, one thousand three, one thousand four), inhale through your nose and fill your lungs completely. Then hold your breath to the count of four (one thousand one, etc.). Now exhale slowly to the count of four. Repeat this deep-breathing sequence eight times. Each time you exhale imagine your muscle tension draining from your body. At this point you should feel very relaxed.

Step 4: Mental Rehearsal.   In this final step of *mental rehearsal* you use your *power of imagination* to reach your chosen goal. You think of *vivid* sensory images relating to your goal. The more real and lifelike the images are, the more effective the exercise will be. Use as many senses and as much detail as possible.

Perform your mental rehearsal through two perspectives. Begin your rehearsal as a *spectator*; that is, view yourself from the outside as you perform your desired goal, as a spectator would view your performance. Then after several replays from a spectator's viewpoint, experience the goal from an internal perspective, as a *participant*. From this perspective, your visual images are no longer from the outside looking in but rather from the inside looking out. As a participant you must also *feel* yourself performing your goal. Again, use images from all your senses if possible.

If you have difficulty seeing yourself perform your desired goal from the spectator viewpoint, imagine someone who has had success. For example, if you want to improve your pivot moves, vividly imagine Kareem Abdul Jabbar scoring on a variety of moves. Then from a participant's viewpoint, imagine *you* are Kareem, smoothly performing various moves. Next, from a spectator's perspective, see *yourself* performing Kareem's moves. Finally, from a participant's viewpoint, look over your shoulder at Kareem and feel your confidence and body sensations as you score on Kareem with your newly acquired moves!

Step 4: Suggestology. In *suggestology*, you simply repeat instructions or positive phrases using subvocalization. The following rules suggested by Ostrander and Schroeder (1979) apply when using this method:

1. Keep your phrases short and specific.
2. Use the first person and present tense. Your sub-conscious takes your instructions literally.
3. Construct positive phrases. Saying "I don't see a white elephant" only brings that image to mind.
4. Say your phrases with meaning and attention.
5. Speak kindly to yourself.
6. Repeat phrases often.

Here are some examples of phrases that follow these rules.

- I dribble by touch.
- I see the whole court when dribbling.
- I fine center on the basket when shooting.
- I watch the ball into my hands when receiving.
- I am calm and confident when shooting free throws.

When using suggestology, it is a good idea to write down three or four specific statements about yourself that are generally related. For example:

- I am aggressive on defense.
- I am alert and ready to help off the ball.
- I have quick feet on defense.
- I talk on defense.

Recite these phrases over and over and after each phrase, use your mental rehearsal techniques to imagine yourself performing each goal. In this way you are using one mental process (imagination) to reinforce the other (verbalization).

Mental Rehearsal/Suggestology Tapes

If you prefer to listen to directions rather than recite them to yourself, you can make your own mental rehearsal/ suggestology tapes that follow the steps outlined previously. The tapes can be directed either toward your power of imagination or your verbal thought processes using the power of suggestion.

To help you understand what these tapes would be like and to help you experience complete relaxation, I have provided a script for your first tape. This script is comprised of only Step 3 activities and does not precede any Step 4 instructions. Because you will be listening to these instructions rather than reciting them, they have been written in second person. Each of your tapes should begin with the following Step 3 relaxation instructions. Speak slowly and distinctly when making the tapes.

> *Begin by sitting in a comfortable chair.*
>
> *Your body and head are in a straight, upright position.*
>
> *Your shoulders are back; your feet are flat on the floor.*
>
> *Inhale: One thousand one, one thousand two, one thousand three, one thousand four.*
>
> *Hold: One thousand one, one thousand two, one thousand three, one thousand four.*
>
> *Exhale: One thousand one, one thousand two, one thousand three, one thousand four.*
>
> *(Repeat this breathing exercise eight times.)*
>
> *Keep your eyes closed.*
>
> *Make yourself comfortable, and relax.*
>
> *As you listen to my voice, pay no attention to any external distractions.*
>
> *My voice is slowly penetrating your subconscious mind.*
>
> *Relax every muscle in your body.*
>
> *Your feet are relaxed. They are warm.*
>
> *Your calves are relaxed. So relaxed. So limp.*
>
> *Your thighs are loose. They feel heavy.*
>
> *They are warm, limp. So relaxed. So comfortable.*
>
> *All the muscles in your legs and feet are fully relaxed.*

Relax your buttocks and hips.

They are warm and at ease.

This pleasant sensation of warmth and relaxation is creeping through the trunk of your body.

You feel so relaxed, so comfortable.

Your eyes are closed. Do not try to open them.

You are completely relaxed.

Your feet, legs, and the trunk of your body are fully relaxed and at ease.

The sensation of warmth and ease is now creeping through your arms and hands.

Your arms and hands are fully relaxed and limp.

Your arms are so heavy.

Make no attempt to move them.

You now feel a warm, pleasant sensation of relaxation extending up into your neck and head.

Your neck and head are fully relaxed.

Your face is relaxed and calm.

You show no expression.

Your entire body is now fully relaxed and limp.

Every muscle, every nerve, every part of your body.

You are in a warm, pleasant state.

Your heaviness is now fading and you are becoming very light, light as a feather.

You now feel like you're floating on a cloud, resting comfortably.

As you rest in comfort, listen to my voice and keep your mind on my instructions.

Think of nothing but what I am saying to you.

My instructions are penetrating your subconscious mind.

Take a deep breath. Relax.

You are falling deeper and deeper into a state of pleasant relaxation.

In this state of pleasant relaxation, your subconscious mind is becoming more and more receptive to my suggestions.

You are totally relaxed and ready to receive my instructions.

At this point you add the Step 4 instructions. The commands you give yourself depend on the goals you set in Step 1. An example of Step 4 instructions follows. The goal for this example is to play better defense. The instructions given here are a combination of imagination and verbalization programming. As you tape the instructions, be sure to give yourself time to see and feel each cue you give.

Begin by visualizing yourself playing defense with proper stance and balance.

Your weight is evenly distributed on the soles of both feet.

Your heels are barely touching the floor, and your feet are a little wider than your shoulders.

Your head is directly above the midpoint between your two feet.

Your head is up. Your knees are bent. Your back is straight, and your hips and buttocks are low.

Your hands are ready to deflect any passes.

Every joint is flexed and ready for action.

Your body balance enables you to move quickly on defense.

Your quick feet feel very light.

You slide and glide with tremendous quickness.

Feel your lightning feet slide and glide as you defend your player.

You are now moving quicker than ever on defense.

You are superquick.

Feel the sensations of your lightning-quick feet.

Apart—together. Apart—together. Sliding—gliding.

Sliding—gliding. Apart—together.

Your feet are lightning-quick on defense.

Apart—together. Apart—together. Sliding—gliding.

Now feel yourself sliding quickly in the opposite direction.

Your feet are lightning-quick in either direction.

Feel your feet moving quickly apart and together, apart and together.

Your defensive sliding is so smooth, so graceful, so quick.

For the next few moments, visualize your defensive slide in slow motion.

See and feel your smoothness.

Continue to feel your graceful motion as you visualize your sliding motion at full speed, faster than you've ever moved before.

You enjoy playing defense.

Playing defense is fun because you can shut off your opponent.

You enjoy the challenge it gives you.

You play defense with physical intensity and mental alertness.

You are always anticipating.

You are always ready for moves and plays before they happen.

You are always ready and anticipating.

You enjoy playing defense.

You are an all-round player who enjoys playing both offense and defense.

You have total concentration on defense.

Your visual soft centering enables you to see your player and the entire court in front of you.

Your mind is alert. You are always anticipating.

You play aggressively and cleanly without fouling.

You enjoy playing defense. You enjoy the challenge of defense.

You are an all-round player who enjoys playing offense and defense.

Visualize yourself, right now, playing defense with tremendous intensity.

You are a team leader. You are always talking on defense.

You help your teammates by warning them of screens and potential screens.

You call out switches. You encourage your teammates.

You are a leader on defense.

Take a deep breath. Relax.

Breathe deeply again. Continue to visualize yourself play-ing defense for as long as you wish.

See yourself properly executing the defensive fundamen-tals with maximum quickness.

Visualize yourself playing aggressive, alert, thinking defense before your player gets the ball.

Visualize yourself denying your player the ball.

Visualize yourself ready and willing to help a teammate in trouble.

Visualize yourself as a leader on defense.

Continue this visualization process for as long as you wish.

You are a great defensive player.

You execute the fundamentals with maximum quickness.

You play aggressively, alertly, very intensely.

You are a great defensive player.

You may remain in this pleasant state of relaxation as long as you wish.

You are now physically and mentally refreshed.

The tapes you create can be adapted to pursue any goal—better concentration, improved skill, greater intensity, whatever. Simply begin by using the Step 3 script on relax-ation, and follow it with instructions relating to the Step 1 goal you have selected. Write your own Step 4 scripts like the one I have provided on defensive programming. Then listen to one tape each night before going to bed or at any

other convenient time. By listening to your tapes you'll not only improve your basketball habits, you will also become refreshed and reinvigorated because of your deep relaxation.

Seeing a Better You

The fundamental purpose of the suggestology and mental rehearsal drills is to help you eliminate negative thoughts, whether they be in images or words, and to help you develop a better self-image. You must stop your negative internal dialogue and create the image of the player you want to be. When you do this, you break through the limits that confine your performance to something far below your potential.

Questions for Review

1. Identify four types of conscious awareness.
2. Who uses mental rehearsal?
3. What is mental rehearsal?
4. What is suggestology?
5. Why should you use suggestology?
6. Why should you use mental rehearsal?
7. When and where can you use mental rehearsal and suggestology practice techniques?
8. List the four steps in mental rehearsal training.
9. List the four steps in suggestology training.

chapter 1 5

Mind Games

*I felt I was falling asleep and then all at once some-
thing caught my attention. It was not something
which involved my thought processes; it was not a
vision, or a feature of the environment either, yet my
awareness had been engaged by something. I was
fully awake. My eyes were focused on a spot on the
edge of the chaparral, but I was not looking, or
thinking, or talking to myself. My feelings were clear
bodily sensations; they did not need words. I felt I
was rushing through something indefinite. Perhaps
what would have ordinarily been my thoughts were
rushing; at any rate, I had the sensation that I had
been caught in a landslide and something was
avalanching, with me at the crest. . . . I was, at that
moment, in a most peculiar state of awareness. I was
cognizant of the surroundings and of the mental
processes that the surroundings engendered in myself, yet I was not thinking as I ordinarily think.*
—Carlos Castaneda (1974, pp. 23-24)

Up to this point, we have done a lot of studying and
learning, and it's been work! So now we will take a break
and have some fun. We are going to play games! So don't
be bashful or be a spectator. Get involved! Play the games.
But first one word of warning: At times you may find yourself, like the person in the opening quote, "in a most peculiar
state of awareness . . . not thinking as [you] ordinarily
think."

Three Goals

Although we will have some fun in this chapter, we will
also be pursuing three goals:

1. To improve your mind awareness and mind control.
2. To increase your sensory awareness.
3. To improve the efficiency of your vision.

To achieve these goals, first perform the basic drills to improve your mind awareness and sensory awareness. Then, if you have the necessary equipment, perform the trampoline and balance beam drills. These drills heighten your senses of body awareness and balance, helping you to improve your balance and coordination. The advanced drills enable you to develop your visual control while using your other sensory systems at the same time—a task that is required in basketball.

Drilling Ideas

You can use these drills to suit your own particular needs. If you are especially weak in one area, such as balance, you should do additional drills on the balance beam and trampoline. If you lack coordination, you should do the trampoline and floor drills. However, because proper visual awareness is so important in basketball, you should direct most of your training toward increasing visual efficiency. But you should try to increase your awareness and efficiency in all the areas.

Basic Drills

The purpose of the basic drills is to increase your mind awareness and your sensory awareness. They can be done almost anywhere and require no equipment.

Drill 1: Changing Channels. The purpose of this drill is to develop your mind awareness. In this drill simply switch your focus of attention from one system to another as if you were changing the channels on your television set. Focus on the sensations or images of one system for only a few seconds, then switch to a new channel. Refer to the mind dial in Figure 15.1 if necessary.

If this drill is difficult for you now, don't be discouraged. It will become easier after performing the other drills listed.

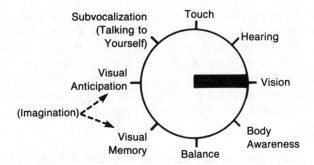

Figure 15.1 Select your sensory channel using the mind dial as a guide.

Drill 2: Silencing Subvocalization. Your task is to silence your inner voice. You must think without words. If a word or phrase pops into your head, try again. It may help to tune in to one of your other mind channels; focus on the sensations of one of your senses. Be careful not to make word associations. Try not to think of the word *ball* when you see a ball. Do this for one minute.

Time's up! How did you do? [Say, "Great!"] Good! Now the drill becomes more difficult. Try to silence your inner voice while reading this page. Start at the top and try to read the whole page without saying the words to yourself. Speed readers employ this trick as they learn to center in their visual system. They do not slow themselves down by saying words or phrases. Many can read well over 1,000 words per minute with comprehension because they read as fast as their vision permits. When you read in this manner your word processing occurs on a subconscious level. Try it; read this page without subvocalizing.

Drill 3: Imagination. Close your eyes and focus on the visual images you bring to mind. Use your visual memory to imagine your last game or practice, or picture yourself in your next game sinking two game-winning free throws. Repeat this drill for a few minutes before continuing.

Drill 4: Visual Awareness (Soft and Fine Centering). Locate any four small objects around you and soft center on all of them. Try to see all four objects at one time without being concerned about picking up detail in any one of them. Then have someone call out the name of one of the four objects.

When the object is called, shift your eyes and fine center on the object without moving your head. Concentrate only on that object and try to notice as much detail as possible. Call out another object and fine center on it. Have your assistant occasionally ask you to soft center so you must shift from fine centering on one object to soft centering on all of them. If no one else is available, you can direct this drill yourself.

Drill 5: Visual Awareness (Soft and Fine Centering). Visually center on an object that is broad yet has a lot of detail, such as a bookcase. First, soft center on the entire bookcase. Then shift to a finer degree of centering by focusing on the top shelf. Next, shift to an even finer degree of centering by focusing on one of the books on the shelf. Fine center even more by picking out the first word in the title of the book. Then continue to narrow your focus of attention by centering on the first letter of the first word of the title. Quickly change back to soft centering on the entire bookcase. Finally, shift to a softer degree of centering by focusing on the entire wall or background behind the bookcase.

Drill 6: Visual Awareness (Ignoring Distractions). Practice Drills 4 and 5 on visual fine and soft centering while waving your hand in front of your face. You must overcome the tendency to follow your hand and must keep your concentration on the designated object. This drill in particular will help you to maintain the focus necessary to see through the hand in your face when shooting.

Drill 7: Hearing (Soft and Fine Centering). Focus your attention on hearing. Begin by soft centering on as many of the sounds in your environment as possible. Try to be aware of many sounds at the same time. Now focus on the loudest or most obvious sound. Next, focus your attention on a subtle noise or sound. If there is no subtle noise, create one by tapping your finger lightly on this book. Focus totally on this subtle sound until you are not aware of the other distracting noises in your environment. This drill helps you to focus on verbal instructions from your coach or a teammate during competition in a noisy environment.

Drill 8: Touch (Soft and Fine Centering). In the previous drill, if you were totally centering on the sound of your tapping finger, you were probably unaware of the touch sensations your mind received from your tapping finger. In this drill, begin tapping your finger lightly as before but this time focus your attention on the sensitivity of your fingertip rather than on the noise generated. Do this for a moment and notice when your mind slips from one focus of attention (touch) to another (hearing).

Now shift your attention from fine centering on your fingertip to soft centering on your entire body. If you are wearing a long-sleeved shirt or sweater, focus on the feel (touch) of your shirt as it clings to your arms and back. Can you feel the touch sensitivity of your arms, wrists, back, shoulders, and chest all at once?

Shift your focus again. If you are sitting, focus on your rear end. If you are standing, focus on the bottom of your feet. Were you aware of these body parts 10 seconds ago? Of course not, even though sensations or signals from these parts were entering your mind. Why were you unaware of them? Because your mind can only center on one system at a time. As you tune in to one channel, you tune out the others. You still receive information from these other systems but only on a subconscious level.

Now take a moment to focus on your touch (tactile) memory. Do you remember how a basketball feels? Do you remember how it feels to receive a pass?

Drill 9: Body Awareness (Soft and Fine Centering). Let's begin this drill by fine centering on various muscle groups. First, flex the biceps (upper arm muscles) of your right arm. Contract the muscle as much as possible for 5 to 10 seconds. Now extend your right arm, stretching your bicep as much as possible. Let your arm hang limp. Did you notice any difference in sensations?

Now contract the quadriceps (upper thigh muscles) in your right leg by extending your leg in front of you. Hold your contraction for a few seconds. Do you feel any muscles stretching in the back of your leg as you do this? Do you feel the tension in your quads?

Stand up and perform your shooting motion for a free throw. Close your eyes and soft center your attention on your entire body. Notice your rhythm from the bend in your knees to the hook on your follow-through. Does your motion seem smooth and flowing or abrupt and jerky? Perform your free-throw motion five or six times paying attention to your sense of body awareness. Then try this same exercise with the mechanics of other basketball skills such as dribbling, defense, and so forth. Use your sense of body awareness to scan your body for tense muscles, stretched muscles, and relaxed muscles.

Drill 10: Balance.   For this drill you must stand up. Put all your weight on one leg so you are standing on one leg. Now lean forward as far as possible while keeping your balance. Hold this position for a second or two and then lean backwards as far as possible. Next, lean to one side and then the other as far as you can without falling. In this drill you should notice the limits of your balance and how you shift your limbs to compensate for leaning in each direction.

Now practice your defensive stance. Are you balanced or leaning forward? Perform your free-throw motion. Are you balanced or leaning forward? What happens to your focus of attention during a game when you are shooting a free throw and you lean too far forward?

Summary.   These basic drills increase your sensory awareness and mind awareness. Your increased awareness helps you to develop your basketball skills at an accelerated rate and to improve your game concentration.

Balance Beam Drills

The purpose of the balance beam drills is to put you in a situation in which your awareness of body balance increases. In this special environment you must react to changes of balance on a subconscious level while centering on your vision.

The heightened sensitivity to balance is something you learn to overcome with practice. Improved balance is especially helpful in shooting and rebounding. Players who can cope with changes in balance while driving to the basket, pulling up for a jump shot, or reaching for a rebound are able to maintain the proper focus of attention on either the basket or the ball, regardless of the situation.

When performing any of the balance beam drills, remember that **safety comes first**! These drills require no heroic action. If you lose your balance, simply step off the beam and start over. Remember, the beam you will be performing on is only 6 to 8 inches off the floor (see the

diagram in chapter 3, "Skill and Body Awareness"). *Do not* attempt these drills on a standard gymnastics beam, which is approximately 3 feet off the floor. If you follow these precautions you are less likely to get hurt.

Of course, the drills included in this chapter are not the only drills available to develop your balance and concentration. Use your imagination to create your own drills. The drills described here simply serve as illustrations. They are ones that I have found to be useful in helping young athletes.

Balance Beam Drill 1. Walk the beam forward and backward centering on your sense of balance. At first use your eyes to watch the beam. After you become comfortable and confident, walk along the beam with your eyes up. Try performing basic Drills 4 and 5 described on pages 161-162 as you walk the beam.

Balance Beam Drill 2. Any time you perceive a threatening situation (even mildly threatening like walking a balance beam or receiving a flu shot), you tense up a little. Check this out for yourself. As you stand or walk on the beam, focus your attention on body awareness. Are you more tense than usual? Probably, as most beginners are. Your increased tension, however, does not necessarily result from fear of injury. It can result from fear of failure, even the trivial failure of not keeping your balance. This drill helps you to learn to read and control your tension level and to develop your balance.

Balance Beam Drill 3.   While walking forward and backward on the beam, maintain your centering on your sense of touch as you move a basketball around your waist. Feel the weight and texture of the ball as you swing it around your body. By focusing on touch, you transfer your sensitivity to balance to a subconscious level.

Balance Beam Drill 4.   Perform the previous drill except this time maintain your centering in your visual system. As you walk the beam moving the ball around your waist, keep your vision riveted on the rim or on another specific object. The object should be in line with the end of the beam. Repeat this drill with your vision soft centered.

Balance Beam Drill 5.   In this drill, walk the beam while dribbling the ball at your side. Try it first by using your vision to maintain your dribble. Next try it while keeping your eyes fine centered on the basket. Before beginning be sure that the basket is in line with the end of the beam.

Balance Beam Drill 6.   With one end of the balance beam near the basket, walk the beam while holding a basketball above your head. Keep your vision fine centered on the basket. When you get to the end of the beam shoot the ball in the basket (no jump shots!). The purpose of this drill is for you to learn to maintain your concentration on the basket when you are slightly off balance.

Balance Beam Drill 7.   For those of you talented enough to juggle three basketballs, try juggling while walking the beam. If you can spin the ball on your finger, try doing that on the beam. The purpose of this drill is to focus on your vision while maintaining your balance on a subconscious level.

Balance Beam Drill 8.   Perform this drill with a partner. As you walk the beam, play catch with your partner, as he or she stands at the end of the beam or walks along with you. As you walk forward, your partner walks backward. You can make this drill even more difficult by quizzing each other with simple math problems or trivia questions. But remember, the goal is to keep your eyes fine centered on the ball!

Trampoline Drills

Although I believe the balance beam drills are good, I think the trampoline drills are even more helpful. The purpose of the trampoline drills is to put you in a situation in which your sense of body awareness is increased. In this special environment you must maintain the proper visual centering. Besides developing your powers of concentration, trampoline training also develops coordination, balance, and the ability to control your body in the air. It is an excellent means of developing your body awareness.

Some rules are necessary to ensure safety. These trampoline drills should be used *only* on a trampoline in which the bed is ground level or where there is a platform constructed around an elevated bed. You must *always* have spotters. The trampoline can be dangerous if used improperly. So **be cautious** as you perform these drills.

Trampoline Drill 1.   Accustom yourself to the trampoline by simply bouncing. As you gain confidence and control, begin increasing the height of your jump and try to bounce as high as you can *under control.* As in any of these drills, if you begin to lose control, check your bounce by bending your knees as you return to the mat and start over. As you

become familiar with the trampoline, your centering of attention may alternate between body awareness, balance, and vision.

When you first begin these drills, take a moment to center on your tension level. You will probably find your tension level is higher than normal. This increased tension decreases with experience on the trampoline.

Trampoline Drill 2. Perform simple stunts such as knee drops, seat drops, swivel hips, and twists (180°, 360°, 540°, and 720°). For instructions on how to perform these skills, consider checking out a gymnastics book from the library. Twists are especially good stunts for those who play in the low post and must pivot on moves and shots.

Trampoline Drill 3. After trampoline Drills 1 and 2 have become routine, begin performing basic Drills 4 and 5 on pages 161-162 while bouncing and doing the simple stunts. Change your focus of attention from fine centering on a single object such as a ball, to soft centering on several objects. Of course, for safety reasons, you must frequently check your position on the trampoline to remain in the center of the mat as much as possible.

Trampoline Drill 4. While bouncing, play catch with a partner who is standing at one end of the trampoline. You can vary this drill by doing 180° or 360° twists between passes. Or your partner can vary his or her passes, throwing some passes sharply and lobbing others. In fact, high lob passes can be used to simulate rebounds. In this variation, the passer should time and aim his or her pass to force the "rebounder" to reach above his or her head at the top of the jump to snare the rebound. This forces the rebounder to keep his or her vision up and fine centered on the ball. **Never attempt any heroic action** to catch the ball! If a bad pass is thrown, forget it. Simply retrieve the ball and start over.

Trampoline Drill 5. With two partners, each with a ball and stationed on the floor at opposite ends of the trampoline, perform 180° turns while bouncing. Your partners pass the ball to you as you turn in the air to face them on your 180° twists. As soon as you receive the ball in the air, pass it back to the passer before you twist and land for your next bounce.

Trampoline Drill 6.   In the next few drills, you and a partner bounce on the trampoline at the same time. Face each
other from opposite ends of the trampoline. Keep your vision
centered on your partner and alternate your bounce; that
is, when you are landing on the mat your partner should
be at the top of his or her jump. You will learn to regain your
balance when your partner "takes your bounce" (this occurs
when you land almost simultaneously on the mat).

Trampoline Drill 7.   After you become accustomed to bouncing with a partner, grab a basketball and play catch as both
of you bounce. This drill requires you to fine center visually
on the ball while your mind is receiving increased sensory
input from your senses of body awareness and balance.
Again, if either you or your partner begin to lose control,
check your bounce and start again. Remember, **no heroic
action**!

Trampoline Drill 8.   When passing to a partner becomes
easy, try this two-player tipping drill. As you reach the
height of your bounce, tip the ball to a point where your partner can tip the ball back at the height of his or her jump.
The trick to performing this drill well is to time your bounce
with your partner's so that you are landing while your partner is at the top of his or her jump. See how many tips you
can make in a row as a team before missing.

Trampoline Drill 9.   With one person bouncing on the trampoline and one person standing at each end (about 1 foot
beyond the trampoline frame), play "monkey in the middle." The two players off the trampoline try to pass the ball
over or around the person in the middle who must try to
deflect the pass. The passers should stay in the middle of
their end of the trampoline and should not wander to the
corners of the tramp so that the middle player has a fair
chance of deflecting the pass. Again, **do not attempt heroic
interceptions**.

Trampoline Drill 10.   Repeat Drill 9, except this time with
two monkeys-in-the-middle working together as a team.
This drill forces the two passers to be soft centered in their
vision as they must be aware of both the middle players and
their partner. The passers may wander the width of the

trampoline bed but may not go beyond the end of the trampoline frame. The two passers attempt to make 10 good passes before switching with the players on the trampoline. The middle players must try to deflect as many passes as possible before 10 good passes are made. After three rounds, the team with the most deflections wins.

Trampoline Drills Summary. The trampoline drills help you develop your sense of balance, body awareness, coordination, and visual concentration. I recommend using them as part of an off-season program. With an attitude of **safety first**, you minimize the risk of injury.

After working with athletes for several off-seasons, I have never had an athlete experience a serious injury on the trampoline. This is primarily because the trampoline bed was ground level. I do not recommend these drills for use on an elevated bed unless a platform is built around it. I also frequently remind the athletes that these drills require no heroic action, and of course, I allow absolutely no horseplay. As a final note, once an athlete overcomes his or her initial fears of the trampoline, he or she often finds these drills to be great fun.

Summary

The mind games described in this chapter are designed to meet several goals. First, the basic drills help you to develop the master sense, mind awareness. Second, they also increase your sensory awareness. The drills on the balance beam and trampoline develop your balance, coordination, visual control, and body awareness. If you expect to improve your mental powers, you must practice them. You must drill for skill!

Questions for Review

1. What is the purpose of the mind games presented in this chapter?
2. What safety precautions should you follow when performing drills on the balance beam?
3. What are the necessary precautions for the trampoline drills?

part 5

Fourth Quarter:
Game Fundamentals

chapter 16

Pressure and the Emotional Elements of Sports

> Physical abilities are relatively equal at the top of
> professional sports. On the Celtics, we believed the
> principal difference between good teams and great
> ones was mental toughness: how well a team could
> keep its collective wits under pressure.
> —Bill Russell (Russell & Branch, 1979, p. 126)

Sports have an amazing impact on our society; in fact, Americans are obsessed with sports at all levels of competition. Our obsession ranges from active involvement in highly organized scholastic and park district programs to passive participation as spectators. What is the great attraction to sports?

Our obsession with sports is partly due to the physical stimulation that sports provide. Exercise makes us feel good. There is also the mental stimulation of sports. We love to plan strategies and second-guess the strategies of others. But perhaps the greatest stimulation we receive is the emotional excitement sports provide. Sports arouse us. They elevate our spirits to great heights. They can also drag us down to the depths of disappointment and depression. Emotionally, sports dramatically affect our lives.

Because of the emotional elements of sports, one of the greatest challenges of competitive athletics is the ability to play consistently at just the right level of physical and emotional arousal. But because of mental and emotional undertraining in athletics, few players are able to compete in game after game at peak levels of performance. Most athletes suffer from either the inability to control their overexcitement while competing or the inability (or unwillingness) to play with enough excitement. In fact, some athletes are so inconsistent in this area that their performance is mediocre one night because they're too tight and the next night because they're not excited enough. The truth is that very few athletes have been trained to develop optimum emotional arousal.

To help you deal with basketball's difficult emotional elements, this chapter discusses the problems of emotional stress and tension and the pressures of competitive basketball that lead to stress. The next chapter, "Coping With Competition: The ABCs," introduces strategies for maintaining the optimum levels of emotional arousal necessary during competition for peak performance.

Levels of Arousal

Our emotions can put us on one of three levels of arousal or excitement. The emotional and performance effects of the three levels are compared in Table 16.1. The emotions of fear, anxiety, anger, and frustration, which can be considered the "hot" feelings, produce a state of overarousal. This overexcitement can dramatically interfere with perfor-

Table 16.1 Levels of Arousal

Level of Arousal	Emotional State		Effect on Performance
Overarousal	"Hot" feelings	Fear Anxiety Anger Frustration	Negative
Optimum arousal	"Warm" feelings	Security Passion	Positive
Underarousal	"Cool" feelings	Apathy Indifference Powerlessness Depression	Negative

mance. On the other hand, depression and the "cool" feelings of apathy, indifference, and powerlessness produce a state of underarousal. This underarousal can also dramatically interfere with performance by making you play at a less than peak level of emotional excitement. The most productive level of arousal lies between the two states of underarousal and overarousal. It is produced by the "warm" feelings of security and passion. The peak performer plays the game in a positive emotional state, feeling secure but driven with passion! He or she is excited by competition but not overexcited by fear, anxiety, anger, or frustration.

Composure in athletics, one of the Three Cs of peak performance, does not mean being unexcited. A lack of excitement is the state of apathy. Composure means being in control of your emotions and excitement; not being overexcited by fear, anxiety, anger, or frustration; nor underexcited because of depression, apathy, indifference, or a sense of powerlessness. Composure is the ability to maintain the warm, positive passion of peak performance. If an athlete cannot maintain his or her composure during competition, he or she will likely suffer the detracting physical and mental symptoms of overarousal.

Overarousal

The bodily changes that you experience when you perceive a threatening or stressful situation, whether it is in athletics or any other area of your life, are known as the fight-or-flight syndrome. This syndrome is a natural phenomenon that literally prepares your body for fighting or fleeing. The mechanics of fight or flight are simple. When you are faced with a stressful situation, your brain sends a signal to your pituitary gland that in turn stimulates the adrenal glands to secrete hormones. These hormones prepare your muscles for action. Your muscles tense, your heartbeat and breathing speed up, your blood flows from your skin and extremities to your large muscles, and your digestive system shuts down.

As a general rule, these physiological symptoms occur in proportion to the *perceived* threat. If you are faced with a true life-or-death situation, your physiological reactions are extreme. However, if the situation is only a mildly threatening siutation involving merely the possibility of embarrassment, for example, then the fight-or-flight symptoms are much milder. In athletics, we rarely, if ever, experience the extreme symptoms of the fight-or-flight syndrome. However, even the slightest symptoms of the fight-or-flight response can negatively affect athletic performance.

Fight-or-Flight and Performance

As anxiety and muscle tension increase they begin to disrupt your coordination and timing. The smooth and intricate contracting and relaxing of your muscles gets out of sequence, and your movements become abrupt and jerky. Your muscles become knotted, and you cannot extend them fully. This restricts your follow-through. Even for the most gifted athlete, the fight-or-flight response, however slight, takes its toll, interfering with relatively simple, overlearned movements such as dribbling.

Not only does your performance suffer because the heightened muscle tension interferes with your skills, but you are also mentally distracted by these bodily reactions because they are so abnormal. They literally compel you to focus on your body instead of the essential visual information. As a result, your visual field is very narrow. In almost every case the overaroused athlete suffers from tunnel vision. The point is that in order to concentrate and to execute your moves with precision, you must be relaxed. Relaxation, concentration, and execution go hand in hand. You can only meet basketball's many challenges by staying mentally and physically relaxed.

On the other hand, you should realize that these physiological changes are not entirely detrimental if controlled. We must be excited to some degree if we are to meet the physical challenges of athletic competition. However, most of us often cross the line of optimum arousal into an overexcited state because of the pressures of the sport itself and the pressure we put on ourselves in the hope of performing well. As a result we experience disrupted concentration and coordination.

Downward Spiral

The mind and body, the mental and the physical, are intertwined. Mental stress can cause physical tension and fatigue, and physical tension can cause anxiety. A snowballing or cyclical effect can occur. For example, when a player enters a "big game" feeling tense and anxious and misses his or her first shot, anxiety and tension increase. The increased anxiety over the first missed shot increases the athlete's physical tension, which further interferes with the fine coordination of shooting. The result is a string of missed shots and a bottomless pit of anxiety, tension, frustration, and failure.

Pressure

The roots of emotional stress and its accompanying fight-or-flight response are found in the many pressures confronting the athlete. Among those pressures are the challenges of the game itself, the pressure exerted by the opponent, social pressures, and perhaps most importantly, those pressures we put on ourselves.

What Is Pressure?   Playing your best comes from focusing on the immediate present. You must center your attention on the important cues (ball, basket, teammate, etc.) in a given situation and react only to those cues. Cluttering your mind with worries over what might happen or what happened in the past does you no good in the present. Worrying about what will happen if you miss a clutch free throw or thinking about the crucial turnover you committed simply adds to the information that your mind must process to make a successful play.

For example, imagine yourself standing at the free throw line with no time left on the clock. Your team is down by one point in the championship game. You have just been fouled and are about to shoot a one-and-one. The stands are packed. The noise is deafening. The opponent's fans are behind the basket wildly waving their arms. You are exhausted and almost too weak to lift your arms. You feel your hands dripping with perspiration as you walk to the bench for a towel. Your coach stands up, walks over to you, and says, "Relax! We need these!" Then your teammates encourage you, "You can do it!" This prompts you to say to yourself, "I can't let them down." After toeing the free throw line you look up and spot the television camera under the basket pointing your way with its red light on. You freeze momentarily as you envision the millions of fans at home watch-

ing you prepare to shoot. As you reach down to touch your toes, your mind flashes a replay of a moment ago when you made one free throw (a brick off the glass) and threw up an air ball on the second. The referee is about to hand you the ball when your opponent suddenly calls time out. You jog briskly back to the bench passing the media table where you hear the television commentator say, "Smitty's been an excellent free throw shooter this season—until today." Instantly, tomorrow's headlines flash in your mind: "**SMITTY BLOWS THE GAME! Substitute Chokes.**" You feel pressure, and most of it is self-imposed.

Is Pressure Beyond Your Control?   It's hard to imagine an athlete having any more pressure than that just described, with the possible exception of a Roman gladiator who could interpret "do or die" quite literally. However, the situation itself does not produce the pressure. Your *reaction* to an important situation creates pressure. The pressure is not external; it is all in your mind. In that sense it is not real.

For example, the task at hand is to make two free throws, one at a time. To accomplish this task you must go through a normal free throw shooting routine (see chapter 7, "Free Throw Funda*mental*s"). Begin with the relaxation exercise, take a deep breath, and exhale. As you take the ball from the referee, line your feet up on the line, bounce the ball once or twice, center your attention in your visual system, and fine center on the basket. Just before shooting, visualize the ball going through the basket to give your mind a positive image. Then prepare, shoot, and follow through. If your regular free throw-shooting routine includes these steps, you should feel no pressure. You just *do it! You* are in control. The only pressure is that which *you* add to the situation. You create pressure by recalling negative experiences or negative results of failure. These thoughts raise you to a higher level of intensity than the "4" level that is necessary for best results.

Admittedly, overcoming pressure is difficult when many distractions (crowd, body tension, past failure, opponent) are clamoring for your attention. However, if you focus on these distractions rather than ignore them, you only add to the pressure. In short, *pressure is increased by the unimportant, negative, or irrational thoughts and feelings that come to mind when confronted with a task.* As in the preceding example, a simple task like making a pair of free throws becomes more than making a pair of free throws. It becomes the game, the season, your ego, your life! Pressure results from letting something be more than it is. In other words, *pressure is something you put on yourself.*

Four Sources of Pressure

There are four sources of pressure in basketball. They include the challenges of the game itself; the pressure put on by the opponent and opposing fans; the pressure we put on ourselves; and social pressures including those exerted on us by parents, friends, fans, and society at large.

The Game Itself.   The first source of pressure is part of the game itself. Basketball requires you to perform skills such as ball handling, shooting, and rebounding, and to play by the rules, execute strategies, and overcome fatigue. These challenges themselves are not great obstacles but are nonetheless sources of pressure, even to an experienced player. A player also experiences some anxiety because of the *uncertainty* of success and the element of luck.

Pressures of Competition.   The second source of pressure is the opponent and the element of competition. This means that in addition to the physical challenges mentioned above, there is the additional challenge of playing better than someone else—your opponent. Your opponent is not only trying to play his or her best, he or she is trying to make you play poorly.

Pressure from your opponent takes several forms. First, it can be *physical*. Your opponent might play aggressively and force you to play more intensely or quickly than optimum intensity or speed requires. Second, pressure can be *mental*. Your opponent might force you to react to changing strategies of offense and defense. Third, pressure can be *moral*. Your opponent might overplay you and double-team you so that you must take bad shots unless you are willing to pass the ball unselfishly to the open player. Finally, pressure can be *psychological*. Your opponent might verbally challenge you to do things that are not strategically sound percentage basketball. For example, if you are a poor outside shooter and your opponent taunts you into shooting from long range, he or she has taken advantage of your ego. The more your opponent taunts, the more psychological pressure he or she puts on you.

Opposing fans can apply many of the pressures that your opponent does. They can apply mental pressure by destroying your concentration with noise, arm waving, and other distractions. They can also apply pressure psychologically through posters and banners that challenge you to do things you cannot do well or to play too intensely by charging you up emotionally. Some fans even resort to annoying, dangerous pranks like throwing coins or other small objects.

Personal Pressure.   The third source of pressure is personal pressure or the pressure you put on yourself. This type of pressure is perhaps the most influential. The glory of victory is a goal deeply embedded in our psyche. Everyone respects a winner. Many envy and adore them; some even look at champions as gods. That is why sports attract us. We like the activity. We love the fun and action and enjoy the challenge. We dream of glory and crave the social rewards and recognition that accompany sports. Our egos inflate with success and deflate with failure, creating a psychologically dangerous situation. If you consider success in basketball the whole basis of your identity and self-worth, then you are putting enormous emotional pressure on yourself. This emotional pressure gnaws at your concentration, composure, and confidence on the court. Success actually becomes more difficult to attain, and the game becomes more than simply a game. It becomes your whole life. As a result, a shooting slump is not *just* a shooting slump—it is slow death. That is *pressure.*

Social Pressure.   Personal/emotional pressure is magnified by parents, friends, fans, teammates, and coaches who consider themselves "stockholders" in your glory. They believe that their attachment to you, whatever it is, is their right to share in your glory. They push you to do better, to win, to gain more glory, because then they themselves will receive a bigger "dividend" of glory. Perhaps the stereotypical Little League father and the stage mother best illustrate this attitude.

Overarousal Wrap-Up

Pressure in basketball is nothing more than the distracting thoughts that enter your mind when confronted with a task. Sometimes it results from forces outside ourselves, but usually pressure results from making the game or situation more important than it is. The sources of pressure are the game itself; the opponent; the opposing fans; your parents, friends, fans, the media, coaches; and perhaps most of all, *you!* Pressure can be physical, mental, moral, personal, and social, and its effects vary with the difficulty of the task. In the next chapter, we study ways to cope with the pressures of basketball by putting the game in perspective with a philosophical understanding of participation and success. *You must have balance and perspective in life to be relaxed and confident on the court.*

Underarousal

Your performance can be affected quite differently by the overarousal symptoms of the fight-or-flight syndrome. It can suffer from underarousal or a lack of excitement during competition. The problem of underarousal and its chief symptom of low emotional energy are due to depression. An athlete's depression is usually brought on by one or more irrational beliefs underlying the feelings of apathy, indifference, and powerlessness.

Depression

Depression in an athlete is exhibited by sluggish movement and low energy levels. It is just the opposite of the highly energized state that the peak performer experiences. Its effects involve more than low energy; research (Durden-Smith & de Simone, 1983) has shown that depression impairs skills as well.

In addition to the physical symptom of low energy levels, depression can also affect the athlete's concentration. As opposed to the very narrow focus of attention created by the overarousal of the hot feelings, the cool feelings of apathy, indifference, and powerlessness create a broad, unfocused attention span. The underaroused athlete is easily distracted by his or her surroundings and does not have the sharp focus of attention needed for shooting, passing, and receiving.

Apathy. Apathy is the feeling of unconcern or insensitivity exhibited by a "so what?" attitude. It is a reaction to the pain or expectancy of failure whereby an athlete, to avoid the pain, becomes desensitized to the outcome of his or her performance. The more a player loses or otherwise fails, the more he or she tries to ignore the "agony of defeat." This growing insensitivity brings on depression.

Indifference. Indifference, like apathy, is a feeling of unconcern exhibited by an "I don't care" attitude. The difference between indifference and apathy is that the indifferent athlete truly does not care about his or her performance whereas the apathetic athlete does not *want* to care and so represses the pain of failure. Although the indifferent athlete does not experience the apathetic athlete's "agony of defeat," neither does he or she experience the peak performer's "thrill of victory." Like the apathetic athlete, the indifferent athlete is mildly depressed and his or her performance suffers as a result.

Powerlessness. Powerlessness is the feeling in which the athlete *wants* to win or succeed but feels that he or she is truly *incapable* of success. This feeling that "I *can't* win!" also creates depression, which in turn detracts from the athlete's performance potential.

Underarousal Wrap-Up

The cool feelings of apathy, indifference, and powerlessness negatively affect the athlete's performance because they bring on depression. The depressed athlete's underarousal makes him or her less able to cope with the game's physical and mental challenges.

Coaches' Corner

Coaches have a tremendous influence over their players. A coach, therefore, must control his or her own emotions during the heat of competition. If players sense that their coach is losing composure, the players are more likely to lose their composure, too. If the coach becomes angry and overaroused because of the officiating, for example, the players also are more likely to become overaroused. If the coach appears to lose confidence, the players will begin sliding into an underaroused state. If the coach seems overly anxious about an important game, the players are more likely to be vulnerable to anxiety. In short, coaches must be the picture of calm in the most stressful situations, and they must also be ready to encourage optimal intensity when necessary.

Coaches must also realize that their emotional displays might create the opposite reaction in their players. When a coach becomes angry in a practice or game and vents his or her anger on a player or the team, the victim(s) of the rage might become apathetic or resentful, especially if they feel the coach's wrath is undeserved. Such apathy and resentment in turn often result in depression, thus creating a motivation problem for the coach.

In brief, when it comes to composure coaches must practice what they preach. If they want their players to stay relaxed or play with intensity, they must be ready and able to act as role models for their athletes.

Summary

One of the great attractions sports have for participants and spectators is the emotional excitement sports provide. The emotional element creates a tremendous challenge for athletes. To perform near your potential, you must play at an optimum level of physical and emotional arousal. This can be difficult to do because of competition's various pressures that provoke the hot feelings of fear, anxiety, frustration, and anger. These feelings pump you up to an overaroused state that negatively affects your skills and concentration.

Your performance can also suffer because of under-arousal or a lack of excitement. This state of depression stems from the cool feelings of apathy, indifference, or a sense of powerlessness. The effects of depression on your performance include sluggish movement, low energy levels, impaired skills, and easily distracted attention. In the next chapter, we discuss proven techniques for coping with pressure and the emotional elements of competition.

Questions for Review

1. What are the three levels of emotional arousal? What emotions and feelings are associated with each level? How does each level of arousal affect performance?
2. What is composure? How is composure different from apathy?
3. What is the fight-or-flight syndrome?
4. What happens to an athlete's performance when he experiences the symptoms of fight-or-flight?
5. Define pressure.
6. Name four sources of pressure.
7. How does depression affect performance?
8. What feelings bring about depression?

chapter 17

Coping With Competition: The ABCs

But contrary to what people think, a self-motivated athlete is rarely one who "eats, sleeps and drinks" his sport to the point that all his self-worth, and even his self-respect, depend on his performance. The all-consuming players value themselves as people only because they play ball. Now if that's the case you'd expect them to play their hearts out, right? Wrong. They don't, because such players usually don't like themselves. They choke, or complain or have strange things going on inside their heads that injure their performance.
—Bill Russell (Russell & Branch, 1979, p. 147)

Basketball is perhaps the greatest of our spectator sports. For the fan, it provides exciting action, an analytical interest in the strategy, and the artistic beauty of the performances. Yet a true appreciation of the game, as of all competitive athletics, is experienced only by actively participating in competition. When watching an athlete or group of athletes perform, you are really witnessing only a very small part of the human experience. You see only the objective reality—the graceful move, the absorbed look of concentration, the all-out hustle, and the emphatic expression of emotion. When participating, however, you discover the entire human experience of sports. You are able to go beyond the objective reality and experience the subjective essence of sports—the attitudes, feelings, emotions, and sensations of athletic competition.

If you are to approach your full potential as an athlete, you must begin dealing with your own subjective reality in the competitive situation. *You* must begin examining very carefully *your* total experiences as an athlete. Your exploration must extend deep below the surface, beyond the objective reality of the physical variables, such as mechanics, form, and technique, that are parts of the competitive equation. You must honestly examine the equally important variables of attitudes, beliefs, feelings, and emotions.

In the last chapter we began considering the mental variables of athletics. We started by examining the emotional elements of sports and their effects on athletic performance. Then we began to expose the underlying beliefs or pressures that provoke emotions dictating the athlete's arousal level and hence affecting his or her performance.

In this chapter you will learn how to explore below the surface of your athletic experience. You will learn to cope with the competitive aspects of basketball by dealing directly with your attitudes and beliefs about the game. Your key to success in this self-examination is a relatively new and simple approach to self-help psychology called Rational-Emotive Therapy or RET (Ellis & Becker, 1982).

The ABCs of RET

Rational-Emotive Therapy (RET) is, as the name implies, a method for *coping with emotional stress through rational thinking*. The RET approach is so simple that a coach or athlete does not need to know very much psychology to help himself or herself deal with the emotional stress of competitive athletics. All they need is a willingness to follow the simple ABCs of RET.

The basic principle of RET psychology is the understanding that our emotional behavior and actions do *not* directly result from the circumstances and pressures of our life situations. We do not respond at point C only because of something that happened to us at point A. The *Activating Event* or *A* (shooting the potential game-tying free throw) does not, by itself, cause our emotional *Consequence* or *C* (overexcitement triggering the fight-or-flight response and distracted attention). Rather, RET psychologists tell us that what happens to a person at point C is profoundly influenced by their *Beliefs* at point *B* (what they tell themselves about point A). In other words, *things are neither good nor bad,*

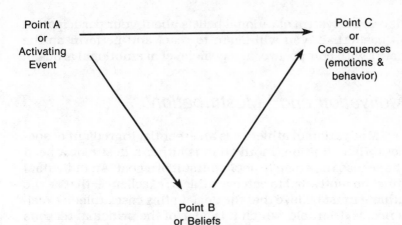

Figure 17.1 The ABCs of RET.

only thinking makes them so. This relationship is illustrated in Figure 17.1.

Most of the time, however, our thinking is so automatic that we do not realize that it is our system of beliefs, not the situation itself, that has triggered our emotional and behavioral reactions. We are conscious of only the A and the C, whereas our B lies hidden in our subconscious.

Rational Versus Irrational Beliefs

The secret to RET begins with the realization that you have two different types of beliefs: *rational* beliefs that help you experience appropriate consequences (feelings of passion, security, peak arousal); and *irrational* beliefs that cause you to experience inappropriate consequences (feelings of anxiety, fear, anger, or frustration that lead to overarousal; or feelings of apathy, indifference, or powerlessness that lead to underarousal). Although you cannot always control or influence the Activating Events (As) in your life, you can almost always influence and control your Beliefs (Bs) that directly lead to your emotional and behavioral Consequences (Cs).

Understanding your beliefs is not easy. Although identifying the As and Cs in your life is fairly simple, identifying your beliefs and changing irrational beliefs into rational ones are much more difficult. Nevertheless, if you work hard to develop a system of rational beliefs about your participation in basketball, you will begin to react and perform on the court with composure, at a peak level of emotional arousal.

Motivation and "Musturbation"

Motivation in athletics is an essential ingredient of success. By definition, motivation is either a desire or a need that causes a person to act in pursuit of a goal. An individual must be motivated to achieve athletic excellence; that is, the athlete must believe that the goal, in this case athletic excellence, is desirable, which it is. One of the principal reasons for participating in competitive athletics is the potential for developing self-esteem. We all have a strong desire to feel good about ourselves. Success in athletics gives us self-esteem.

Motivation, however, can become a problem when an athlete's rational wishes, wants, and desires become irrational necessities or *musts*. For instance, an athlete who becomes all-consuming about his or her sport and believes he or she *must* be highly successful in order to be accepted and appreciated by others, is guaranteeing underachievement, if not failure. RET psychologists suggest that this type of thinking, or "*musturbation*," is the root of almost all emotional evil. They tell us that whenever you are emotionally disturbed—anxious, angry, frustrated, or depressed—you can invariably find a *must* that lies beneath the feelings creating the disturbance (Ellis & Becker, 1982, p. 26). In athletics, almost all emotional disturbances stem from the irrational beliefs based on "musturbatory" thinking.

Pressure and Musturbation

By now, you may have realized how the pressures of basketball discussed in the last chapter and musturbatory thinking are connected. Musturbatory beliefs are irrational simply because they do not help you achieve what you want. Instead they hinder you because of the pressure they create. For example, anytime you tell yourself, "I *must* do well!" rather than "I really want to do well," you create pressure for yourself that shows up in the emotions of anxiety, fear, anger, frustration, and depression. These emotions, as we have learned, lead to either overarousal or underarousal. In either case the effect on performance is negative.

Doing Your ABCs

Coping with competition can be less of a problem when you follow the simple ABCs of RET. When you are about to participate in a highly competitive athletic situation, or when you did not perform up to your expectations because of overarousal and want to know why, take a moment to work out your own personal ABCs.

For the sake of understanding, it may be helpful to combine the images of the letters A, B, and C with the image of an iceberg. Begin by drawing a big A on a sheet of paper. The A, or Activating Event, represents your particular difficulty—competition in general, the big game, a clutch situation, free throws, breaking the press, or some other problem you may be experiencing. Below the A, label the particular problem you want to address (see Figure 17.2).

Problem: Free Throws

Figure 17.2 Doing your ABCs—Step 1.

Next, add the image of the iceberg by drawing the ocean waves separating the tip of the iceberg, Consequences (Cs), from the Beliefs (Bs) existing below the surface as shown in Figure 17.3.

Then, because it is easier to see and recognize the feelings or symptoms existing above the water—the tip of the iceberg—identify the emotional, physical, and mental Consequences (Cs) of your Activating Event (A) as illustrated in Figure 17.4.

Consequences

Beliefs

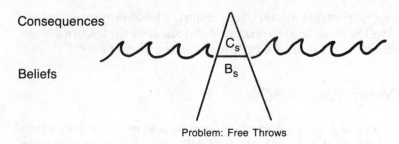

Problem: Free Throws

Figure 17.3 Doing your ABCs—Step 2.

Finally, once you have identified the consequences of your problem, you are ready to explore below the surface to discover the irrational beliefs causing your emotional disturbance. At this point, you must be totally honest with yourself. If you are a "musturbator" who says, "I *must* make these free throws, or people will think I am a rotten player!", then admit it. If you lack confidence in your ability and feel anxious, and you think to yourself (though you may not actually *say* it), "I'm not going to make these. I'm a terrible free throw shooter. I *must* get this over with!", then admit it. Even if your belief is as absurd as thinking that your teammates will never speak to you again because you missed an important free throw, then write down your idea. Whatever irrational beliefs you have, write them down. If you worry about disappointing your teammates and think, "I *must* not

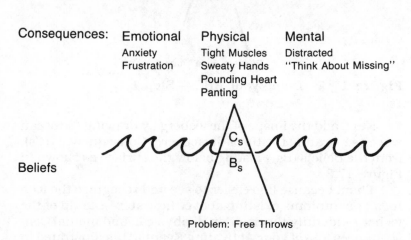

Consequences: | Emotional | Physical | Mental |

Emotional	Physical	Mental
Anxiety	Tight Muscles	Distracted
Frustration	Sweaty Hands	"Think About Missing"
	Pounding Heart	
	Panting	

Beliefs

Problem: Free Throws

Figure 17.4 Doing your ABCs—Step 3.

let my teammates down!'', then express it in writing. Be specific. Only after clearly identifying your hidden, underlying fears and beliefs can you begin to deal with them. Once you expose and express your irrational beliefs, you can destroy them. This is done in the next step of RET—*D* (Disputing your irrational beliefs).

Disputing

Disputing in RET involves applying the scientific method. You propose a hypothesis or theory (your beliefs) and test its validity. In other words, you try to determine whether your beliefs are rational or irrational. The basic question is, ''Where is the evidence that my beliefs are true (rational)?'' Applied to basketball, the question becomes, ''Where is the evidence that I *must* do well in basketball to win the approval of others?'' Or, ''In what way is it *awful* when I do not perform as well as I would like?''

There is no evidence for either the musturbatory thinking or ''awfulizing.'' There is no law of the universe that says you *must* perform well or that it *is* awful if you do not. These beliefs are your own irrational reality. However, because *you* created these beliefs, *you* can change them to reflect a more sensible reality.

Rather than believe you *must* perform well, you can choose to believe that you simply *prefer* or *want* to perform well. Rather than believe it is *awful* when you do not perform as well as you would like, you can choose to believe it is just *unpleasant* or *unfortunate*. By actively disputing your irrational beliefs, you develop a new set of rational beliefs (*B*s) that result in more realistic emotions and reactions (*C*s) to competitive situations (*A*s). Your new sets of *B*s and *C*s will enable you to cope with competition and thereby will improve your performance.

Combating the Causes of Overarousal

Your irrational beliefs can take many forms, but they are primarily the result of a foolish exaggeration of the facts in which you believe your whole self-worth depends upon your performance in basketball. These irrational beliefs usually take the form of personal and social pressure. As you will see, much of the pressure you experience in sports can be eliminated by rationally *disputing* these pressures and exposing their irrational foundations.

Personal Pressure

The personal pressures of the game result from wanting to satisfy psychological drives through basketball. Everyone wants to feel accepted and loved, and everyone enjoys recognition. These desires and drives are natural and healthy. Being accepted and loved gives us emotional security. Aspiring for success provides a challenge. It stimulates us, helps us grow, and makes life more interesting by giving us a goal beyond our grasp. But these desires and drives can be satisfied by means other than basketball. You don't *need* to be Number 1, All-State, All-American, or All-Pro in basketball. Your family, friends, peers—the people close to you—love, accept, and respect you for more than your ability to bounce and toss a ball. Your emotional desires *can* be met by being an All-Pro student, an All-American brother, or an All-World teacher, truck driver, or salesman. John Wooden, whose UCLA Bruins dominated college basketball for more than a decade, once said, "Basketball is not the ultimate. It is of small importance in comparison to the total life we live" (Wooden & Tobin, 1973, p. 91).

The point is that when you make basketball your *whole* life, your *whole* world, your *only* means of satisfying these drives, and the *only* measure of your self-worth, you are overloading yourself with unnecessary pressure on the court. This pressure only increases your anxiety, body tension, and mental stress. The result is a poor performance. In short, the belief that you *must* excel in basketball to be accepted by others is ridiculous and totally irrational.

Complicating the problem of personal pressure is our love of numbers and statistics. We tend to measure success quantitatively. Individuals become obsessed with rebounding and scoring averages, whereas teams and their fans become obsessed with win/loss records and national and state rankings. The obsession with scoring 20 points a game, winning 20 games a season, and being ranked Number 1 adds unrealistic, unnecessary, irrational pressure to teams and individuals. After all, the game is played on the court, not on paper. Rankings are mythical concoctions. Win/loss records are only relative to the quality of competition. Individual statistics are not a true measure of an athlete because many factors influence the numbers. These factors include the quality of the athlete's teammates, the coach's system and philosophy, game tempo, selfish or unselfish play, the opponent's ability, and others. Chapter 23, "Most Valuable Player," presents a realistic set of criteria for evaluating the individual performer. So forget the numbers!

Social Pressure

Just as the chief source of personal pressure is our own egos and insecurity, the chief source of social pressure is the egos and insecurity of others—parents, friends, coaches, and fans. We begin to feel social pressure when others let us know either directly or indirectly that we do not meet their expectations. Often these expectations are unrealistically high as people close to us become caught up in dreams of glory. The solution to social pressure is rational and straightforward behavior. Let others know you are only concerned with doing your best and are committed to doing so. Don't let their overanxiety and preoccupation with dreams of glory interfere with your emotional well-being, on or off the court. When the musturbators around you become too demanding and critical or too disappointed when you miss a free throw, remember, *their* irrational thinking is *their* problem. If they wish to upset themselves over your performance, then they are the ones who must suffer the emotional consequences of their own musturbatory thinking.

In summary, pressure in basketball results from making the game or situation more than it is. It is the outcome of irrational demands that we make upon ourselves. Hence, pressure is something we put on ourselves. Coping with the pressures of basketball is easier when you put the game in perspective with a rational understanding of success and why you participate in basketball. You must have balance and perspective in life to be relaxed and confident on the court.

Treating the Symptoms of Overarousal

So far this chapter has focused on eliminating the causes of overarousal in athletics. Although this is the ideal solution to the problem, coping with competition can be done to some degree by attacking the symptoms of overarousal. In fact, some athletes must treat the symptoms of overarousal (increased muscle tension; shallow, rapid breathing; nausea; and a narrow focus of attention) before they can work out their irrational beliefs and adopt a healthier attitude toward competitive athletics. Also, when an athlete has developed skills in treating the symptoms of overarousal, he or she will be able to use these skills during the heat of competition to enhance his or her performance when it is unclear why the symptoms are occurring.

Reading Your Tension Level

Tension has a way of creeping up on athletes without them realizing its presence. If you are to counteract tension, you must be able to read your tension level first. You must learn to differentiate feelings of tension from those of relaxation. You can perform two simple exercises to help you experience the full tension/relaxation range.

The first is a simple, isometric tension exercise. Begin by tightening all your muscles from head to toe using isometric contractions. Hold your isometric contractions 5 seconds and then gradually exhale and relax. Repeat this procedure three or four times. Notice the extremes of tension and relaxation produced. After doing this four times you should feel very relaxed.

The second thing you can do to experience the full tension/relaxation range is to listen to a relaxation tape. Instructions on how to prepare a tape are presented in chapter 14, "Suggestology and Mental Rehearsal: Easy-Chair Drills." This exercise enables you to experience complete relaxation. By contrasting this fully relaxed state with your normal tension level, you will be able to recognize when your tension level is increasing above normal.

Relaxation Techniques

In addition to learning to read your tension level during competition, you must learn to relax to your normal tension level in just a few seconds. Some people achieve this through training in autogenics, a program designed to enable self-regulation of bodily processes.

This program, designed by Russian researchers, not only helps people to consciously control processes such as digestion, breathing, blood pressure, circulation, and metabolism, but it also helps them to control their emotional states including anger and anxiety. The program involves six steps and requires, according to Garfield (1984), 3 months of short, daily exercises. If you are interested in this training method, I suggest you read *Peak Performance* (Garfield, 1984) or *Superlearning* (Ostrander & Schroeder, 1979).

For most athletes, the four simple relaxation exercises that follow should be enough to overcome heightened anxiety and tension.

Exercise 1: Isometric Tension Adjustment. Before a game, during warm-ups, or during any break in the action, you can reduce muscle tension by a simple, isometric tension-adjustment exercise. While slowly inhaling, flex all the muscles in your body from head to toe. Tense your legs, stomach, arms, face, everything, until you almost quiver from the sheer tension. Then relax completely as you slowly exhale. Do this three times and you should be completely relaxed.

Exercise 2: Deep Breathing. Another way to release tension is by deep breathing. Taking deep breaths and slowing down your breathing rate counters a very annoying physical symptom of anxiety—rapid, shallow breathing. When you practice deep breathing, focus on the rate and depth of breathing. This process helps the diaphragm and the chest muscles relax, allowing fuller, deeper breaths.

To perform the deep breathing exercise you should:

1. Inhale. Breathe in deeply and slowly to a count of four.
2. Hold your breath. Hold it for a count of four.
3. Exhale. Let the air out slowly to a count of four.

Exercise 3: Neck Stretch. The muscles in the back of your neck are among the tightest in your body. You can release much of your physical tension by concentrating on your neck muscles. To perform the neck-stretch exercise you should:

1. Straighten your neck by lessening the normal curve in the back of your neck.
2. Relax your face and jaw allowing your chin to drop toward your chest.
3. Lower your head toward your chest by placing one hand on the top back of your head and gently pulling your head forward and down, but do not actually touch your chin to your chest.
4. In the lowered position, move your head a little to each side keeping your head in each position for 30 to 60 seconds.
5. Return to the vertical position. Then place your left hand on the right, top side of your head and gently pull your head toward your left shoulder stretching the muscles on the right side of your neck. Relax both shoulders and hold that position for 30 to 60 seconds.
6. Repeat the neck stretch to the right side.

Exercise 4: Meditation or Calming Thoughts. The first three exercises induce relaxation from physical to mental. By relaxing your body you eliminate one of the causes of anxiety—excess muscle tension. Because the mind and body are so closely intertwined, by relaxing your muscles you relax your mind as well. But relaxation can also be induced from mental to physical. Using either method, from physical to mental relaxation or vice versa, you can stop and reverse the snowballing effect of anxiety and tension.

This exercise is useful just before a game. Focus your mind on a still object such as the basket. By focusing your mind on that object for a moment, you calm your mind by keeping it free from other disturbing thoughts. You also prepare yourself to apply that same constant focus when shooting during the game.

A second mental relaxation exercise pairs an image with a state of relaxation. University of Illinois Sport Psychologist Dan Smith instructs players to associate a soft color, light blue, with a state of relaxation. He then tells the players to visualize the color light blue whenever they begin to feel anxious during competition. "Light blue" is not a magical image for inducing relaxation. The important point is that the technique of pairing an image with a state of relaxation is valuable in helping to reduce tension by simply thinking about that image during competition. Whatever image you use, whether it be floating on a cloud, stretching out in your favorite easy chair, or some other relaxing image, this technique can have a dramatic calming effect.

Coaches' Corner

Coaches will find the RET approach to emotional problem-solving very useful in counseling anxious athletes. The following example gives coaches an idea on how to handle a delicate situation.

EDDIE: Coach, can I talk to you a minute?

COACH: Sure, Eddie. Come on in. Why don't you close the door and have a seat. What's on your mind?

EDDIE: Well, I just came to tell you I've decided to quit the team.

COACH: Quit? Why do you want to quit?

EDDIE: I don't know. Basketball just isn't any fun any more. I kind of lost interest.

COACH: Are you sure? Have you really thought this out?

EDDIE: Yeah. I've been thinking about this for a few weeks now. I'm just not having fun like I used to. I used to get to play more in games, but now I'm not getting any playing time. Even in practice I don't work much with the first string. And because the team obviously doesn't need me, I thought I should hang it up.

COACH: I see. I'm sorry to hear you feel that way. I have noticed you haven't been playing with your usual spirit. I know it's a tough situation.

Everyone wants more playing time, and I don't blame you. But before we make this final, would you mind doing a little exercise with me—just to make sure this is what you really want to do?

EDDIE: OK.

COACH: Good. Now, you know that mental training book we've been using this season, *Basketball Fundamentals*?

EDDIE: Yeah.

COACH: Why don't we try using the RET approach? In fact, why don't we write out your thoughts on a sheet of paper?

EDDIE: Sure.

COACH: OK, we'll start by drawing our *A* or Activating Event and labeling it—lack of playing time. And for effect, let's draw in the waves so we can distinguish between the tip of the iceberg and what's below the surface. Remember, above the water we're going to put the *C*s or Consequences —your feelings and behavior. Below the water, we're going to put your *B*s or Beliefs. But first, let's start with your feelings or *C*s. If I remember, you said you've lost interest and you're not having fun any more? Is that right?

EDDIE: Yeah, basically.

COACH: OK, let's put this on paper. At the top we'll put "quitting team" as your behavioral Consequence and "depression" and "apathy" as your emotional Consequences. Does this look right to you?

EDDIE: Yeah, I think so.

COACH: Well, what else? There's got to be more to this.

EDDIE: I don't know. I guess that's all.

COACH: What about feeling powerless? You said it didn't matter how you did in practice. Isn't that feeling powerless?

EDDIE: I guess so.

COACH: I also sense from your comment about the team not needing you that you feel a bit worthless. Is that right?

EDDIE: Sort of.

COACH: Uh-huh. Then let's put those down under the Cs also—"powerlessness" and "worthlessness." Does that look right?

EDDIE: That looks about right.

COACH: How about other interests? Do you want to quit because there are other things you want to do instead of play basketball?

EDDIE: No. Not really.

COACH: Is there something outside of basketball that is making you depressed? Or is it basketball in particular that you're depressed about?

EDDIE: No. It's just basketball. It just isn't fun any more. I just don't care to be on the team any more.

COACH: You keep coming back to the fact that it isn't fun any more. Why isn't it fun anymore?

EDDIE: I guess it's just because I don't get to play in games like I used to. I think I'm as good as some of the other guys who are starting but I don't seem to get the chance to show it any more.

COACH: OK, let's leave it at that. In our diagram, we've put the feelings of depression, apathy, powerlessness, and worthlessness up by the Cs.

EDDIE: Yeah.

COACH: OK, we know what's at the tip of the iceberg. And I think I know what's underneath the surface, but let's work out your Beliefs. You can see I've already put one *B* down on the diagram—your Belief that you should be playing more. Also, you said something about being as good as the other guys and you think you should be playing as much as them.

EDDIE: Yeah.

COACH: OK, so we'll put this second idea down. But you know, wanting to quit is pretty drastic action, so my idea is that there has to be a lot more below the surface. In fact, I think your belief is, "I *must* play more in games or being on the team isn't worth it" and, "I *can't stand* seeing others playing ahead of me! I *must* play as much as they do!" Isn't that right?

EDDIE: Yeah, I guess so.

COACH: And didn't you also say that it doesn't matter how well you play in practice, you still don't get the chance you deserve?

EDDIE: Yeah. That's how I feel.

COACH: So in other words, you're saying, "I *must* be treated fairly!" and, "I *must* be given more playing time when I play well in practice!"

EDDIE: Yeah.

COACH: And when you say, "The team doesn't need me," I think you're saying, "In order for me to make a significant contribution to the team, I *must* make my contribution during the games."

EDDIE: You make it sound like it isn't right for me to feel that way, Coach.

COACH: Well, Eddie, it is natural to have the feelings that you have. But maybe not to the degree you feel them.

EDDIE: What do you mean?

COACH: I mean you have a classic case of *musturbation*.

EDDIE: I don't get it.

COACH: It's simple. You've taken an *unpleasant* situation, one in which you should feel disappointed, annoyed, and a bit frustrated and because of your irrational thinking, turned it into an *intolerable* situation in which you want to take the irrational step of wanting to quit the team.

EDDIE: Why is quitting the team irrational?

COACH: Because it is exactly opposite of your real goal—playing on the team. If you were thinking rationally, you would be pursuing your goal with greater motivation. You would be trying harder to make the starting team. But because of your irrational beliefs, you are about to make an irrational decision—quitting.

EDDIE: What's wrong with my beliefs? Why do you say they're irrational?

COACH: I'm glad you asked. Let's look at them and see if we can't dispute them.

EDDIE: OK.

COACH: First, let's start with the belief, "I *must* play more in games or being on the team isn't worth it!" Where's the evidence that this is true?

EDDIE: Evidence?

COACH: Yes, why *must* you play more in games to make your participation worthwhile?

EDDIE: I can't give you reasons. I just feel it.

COACH: Do you believe that playing in games is the only good reason for being on the team?

EDDIE: No, I guess not. I get to exercise playing ball and I'm with my friends. But that's not enough.

COACH: Why isn't it enough?

EDDIE: I don't know. I guess I want to be out there where the action is.

COACH: Game action you mean?

EDDIE: Yeah.

COACH: Well, I can buy that. I would much rather be playing than sitting on the bench. But Eddie, does it make sense to give up two very positive things—getting exercise playing basketball and the comradeship that goes along with it—just because you can't have everything you want?

EDDIE: Maybe not.

COACH: Then think about it. I believe you're giving up a lot by quitting.

EDDIE: Maybe you're right. I don't know.

COACH: OK, let's go to your second belief. "I *can't stand* seeing others playing ahead of me! I *must* play as much as they do!" What do you mean by "can't stand" it? Do you mean you're going to die?

EDDIE: Of course not.

COACH: How *awful* is it? On a scale of 1 to 100, where does it fit in with dying, slow physical torture, falling out of an airplane at an altitude of 10,000 feet, eating the cafeteria food, and the other awful things you can think of?

EDDIE: Well, I guess, it isn't really that awful, and I probably can stand it, but I don't like it.

COACH: Nobody says you have to like the situation or be happy about it. In fact, I would be disappointed if I had a player who didn't want to make the starting team. But not liking something is much different than saying you can't stand it, isn't it?

EDDIE: I guess so.

COACH: Then let's go on to the third belief, "I *must* play more in games or I am worthless!" Notice I've changed this a bit because I think it reflects what you really believe. You not only think you're worthless to the team, but you think *you*, as an individual human being, are totally worthless. Isn't there some truth to this?

EDDIE: Sure. I'm a basketball player. What good is a basketball player who doesn't play?

COACH: Well, first of all, let's look at your idea of being worthless to the team. How good of a team do you think we would be if we only had five players on the team?

EDDIE: Not very good. There wouldn't be anybody to practice against.

COACH: Precisely. That makes every man on the team valuable.

EDDIE: Well, that's true but I still don't feel very good about myself.

COACH: But we haven't got to the most important point. Suppose you weren't on our team. Suppose you played for Youngstown instead. You would probably be a starter for Youngstown, don't you think?

EDDIE: Yeah.

COACH: And if you started for Youngstown, would you then feel you were a worthy person?

EDDIE: Well, not just because of that, but it would make me feel better.

COACH: Yes, you would feel better, but would you be a more worthy person than you are now?

EDDIE: No, I guess not.

COACH: Then does being a starter for Lockport determine whether you are a worthy or worthless person?

EDDIE: No.

COACH: And don't forget, you, Eddie Smith, are more than just a basketball player. You're a good baseball player, a good student, a fine son, and who knows, a potential doctor, lawyer, or top business executive. So does it make sense for you to be depressed about not being a starter on this team?

EDDIE: Not when you put it that way.

COACH: Good. Now let's look at the fourth belief. "I *must* be treated fairly! I *must* be given more playing time when I do well in practice!" Do you really think I'm being unfair about playing time?

EDDIE: Yeah, I think I should be starting ahead of Joe or Pete.

COACH: I'll admit you are a better offensive player than either Joe or Pete. But we already have three good scorers in the lineup. We don't need a fourth scorer as much as we need Joe's defense or Pete's rebounding. I know my reasoning doesn't exactly make you happy, but can you understand my decision?

EDDIE: Yeah. I guess so.

COACH: OK, just so you understand. And who knows? I may or may not be right. I can make mistakes as a human being. But I am doing what I think is best for the team. That's all that anyone can ask. And it's not that you're a bad player, Eddie. You're a good player. I think you have potential to be a *very* good player. Next year as a senior you will probably start. But at this point, you're playing behind three excellent shooters. It's a tough situation for you, I know. The question is, are you willing to go through a little short-term pain for long-term gain? Even though you're disappointed and you believe you're being treated unfairly, are you willing to stick it out and work hard now so that when your opportunity comes next year you'll be ready?

EDDIE: I guess so.

COACH: Then does this mean you are going to stay with us?

EDDIE: Yeah. I feel better now. I still think I should start, but I'm going to stick it out no matter what.

COACH: Good. I'm glad. I think you're making a sensible decision. And who knows, maybe my opinion will change about this year and you'll get a chance to play more. Just keep working hard and trying to do your best. I'm definitely counting on you for next year.

EDDIE: OK. Thanks, Coach.

In this example, you can see how communication and the RET approach can defuse an emotional time bomb ticking away inside one of your players. With a little practice you can make the ABCs work for you.

Summary

An athlete absolutely must learn to cope with the pressures of competition to reach his or her potential. This requires an athlete to be able to deal with emotions and feelings (pressures) that prevent him or her from competing at a peak level of arousal. The most effective way to avoid overarousal or underarousal is to sit down and work out your feelings about competition using the RET approach. You must first identify the *A* or Activating Event causing your emotional disturbance. Second, you must identify your *C*s or emotional and behavioral Consequences. Third, you must identify the irrational underlying *B*s or Beliefs making you emotionally disturbed. Finally, you must *D*ispute your irrational beliefs and replace them with rational ones.

In addition to dealing directly with the causes of overarousal through an RET approach, you can improve your performance by also treating the symptoms of overarousal. You can do this by using four simple relaxation techniques. The first technique is an isometric tension-adjustment exercise in which you tense your muscles for a few seconds and then relax them. The second technique is a simple deep-breathing exercise in which you regulate your breathing by focusing on the rate and depth of your breaths. The third technique is a neck-stretch exercise that loosens the muscles around your neck and shoulders. The last technique uses meditation and image pairing to induce relaxation. These relaxation techniques can be used immediately before a game and during breaks in the action to counteract increasing physical and mental tension.

In both the RET approach and the relaxation techniques, practice is important. You learn and master these competition-coping skills the same way you learned and mastered your dribbling, shooting, and passing skills— through diligent practice. With a little hard work you can master them; when you do you will perform consistently closer to your potential.

Questions for Review

1. What is the basic principle of RET psychology?
2. What do the letters *ABC* represent in RET psychology?
3. Give examples of Consequences of rational Beliefs.
4. Give examples of Consequences of irrational Beliefs.
5. What is musturbation?
6. How does musturbation affect performance?
7. Describe four exercises you can use before and during a game to reduce tension and stress.

chapter 18

Pregame Programming and Postgame Analysis

The situations in which you would want to psych up an athlete are definitely very limited. There is too much psyching-up going on. You should treat arousal like a loaded gun. The athlete who is psyched up is bordering on being out of control. He has a limited control over his attentional processes, so he must rely more on his environment to provide direction. To function effectively, either he must be lucky or the environmental situation must be stable.
—Robert Nideffer (1976, p. 250)

Very often the outcome of a basketball game is determined in the first few minutes of the game or in the first couple of minutes of the second half. How a team plays at the start not only makes a difference in terms of a few points swinging either way, it also affects an entire half or even the whole game because of the momentum created. The early going also generally dictates game strategy and which team will control the tempo. Because of this it is crucial that each player is mentally ready for the beginning of each half. By being mentally prepared you stand a better chance of controlling the game and your opponent. You do this *only* by having a prepared strategy and by being in control of your mind and body before the game.

An example of how one of basketball's top professionals approaches a game might be helpful. David Halberstam describes the pregame ritual of UCLA and NBA star Bill Walton in *The Breaks of the Game*:

> [Walton] loved the day of a game, particularly an important game. It was a time which belonged completely to

*him, a time pure in its purpose. On the day itself he did
not analyze the game, he had done that the night before,
thought about the team and the player he was going
against in the most clinical way possible. The night before
was the analytical time. The day of the game was different. . . . This was the time in which he felt the rhythm and
tempo of the game, almost like feeling a dance of his own.
He played his own music, from the Grateful Dead . . . and
the music helped, it flowed through him and he thought
about the tempo he wanted to set and how he could move.
He would sit in his home or his hotel room in those hours
and actually see the game and feel the movement of it.
Sometimes he did it with such accuracy that a few hours
later when he was on the court and the same players
made the same moves, it was easy for him because he had
already seen it all, had made that move or blocked that
shot. He loved that time . . . he was absorbed in his feel for
basketball. He was amazed in those moments at how clearly
he could see the game, see the spin on the ball and the
angles from which different players were coming. Moment
by moment in that time he became more confident until
when he arrived in the locker room he was absolutely
ready, pumped in his word. There he stayed by himself,
breathing deeply, psyching himself. Lionel Hollins had
loved watching him in those moments, knowing he was
ready, the deeper the breathing the better the omen.
Walton would flex his hands and bounce on the balls of
his feet, like a boxer getting ready for a match. (1983,
pp. 146-147)*

Getting Ready

In this chapter we will look at what you should do to
prepare for a game the few days before, the night before, in
the locker room just prior to the game, and at halftime. We
will also cover the importance of the postgame analysis.

The Few Days Before

Preparing for a particular contest generally starts two
or three days before the game in team practice sessions. The
only exception to this is at the professional level or at tournament time when you are scheduled to play on consecutive
days and have no time to practice between games. In these
practice sessions you must be an earnest student. You must

listen to your coach as he or she goes over the opponent's style, strengths, weaknesses, and individual habits. The knowledge you gain in these practice sessions pays big dividends during the game. As a result of your study, your responses to your opponent's moves are quicker and more automatic. You don't have to spend as much time analyzing on the court; you know which options are high percentage options and which are not. The end result is fewer mistakes on your part and more by your opponent or, in other words, the difference between victory and defeat.

The Night Before

Although some coaches believe it's a good idea to take your mind off the game and get a good night's sleep (the assumption here is that thinking about the game interferes with sleep), I believe you should use mental rehearsal to prepare for your opponent. By combining your knowledge of your opponent with your power of imagination, you acquire a one-step advantage over your opponent in the first few minutes of the game.

A thorough knowledge of your opponent can backfire on you if you don't have the proper attitude. In preparing for competition, you must be neither fearful nor overconfident but simply committed to doing your best. This attitude helps you to play at optimum intensity whether you're playing the NBA All-Stars or the last-place team in the league. When performing mental rehearsal drills the night before the game, do not think entirely of your opponent. Spend time focusing on your own intensity and concentration. After all, you do not want to play their game; you want to play your game.

In the Locker Room

The traditional approach used by coaches in the locker room before a game is to discuss strategy and to give a pep talk. Many coaches even take pride in their ability to charge up their players emotionally. However, as sport psychologists are now pointing out, this "psych job" may do more harm than good. What an athlete needs is *heightened awareness, not heightened emotions.* Heightened emotions typically narrow your focus of attention and interfere with your smooth coordination by increasing muscle tension. If play does not go well right away, your heightened emotion turns into high anxiety and a negative frame of mind. When that happens, the game controls you rather than you controlling the game.

Self-Awareness. The secret to game preparation is self-awareness. Heightened awareness, including self-awareness (mind and body), puts you in control of yourself and the events happening around you. When you step onto the court for the opening tip, you should not focus on the butterflies in your stomach, the tension in your muscles, or the doubts in your mind. You should be relaxed physically with your mind focused on the critical objects for each situation (ball, basket, teammates, etc.), and becoming relaxed is easier through a sense of self-awareness.

Check Points. Self-awareness begins in the locker room with an internal focus of attention. You start with *attitude awareness*. Ask yourself, "Am I worried about the outcome of the game? Or am I going to do my best and take things as they come?" An *attitude check* just before a game reinforces your commitment to playing at optimum intensity right from the start and prevents the danger of overarousal.

After your attitude check, focus internally on *body awareness* for a *body check*. If you are a little uptight physically, perform the relaxation exercises explained in chapter 17, "Coping With Competition: The ABCs."

Finally, do a *mind check*. Focus on your master sense, *mind awareness*. You must prepare yourself to center on your senses, particularly vision. If you do not "come to your senses" and begin talking to yourself on the court while imagining the worst, you weaken your powers of visual awareness. You cannot focus on your senses and talk to yourself at the same time; they are two different mental operations. Remember, proper concentration means focusing on your senses and being locked into the present. You cannot think about the past or the future; you must be in the here and now. Just before the game, practice the visual control drills described in chapter 15, "Mind Games." Most importantly, be sure to spend time changing your visual awareness from soft centering to fine centering and vice versa.

Do *not* perform the suggestology or mental rehearsal exercises just before the game. These exercises are intended to work on your subconscious through the mental processes of verbalization and imagination. Immediately before the game they are counterproductive. A 20- or 30-minute session of mental rehearsal and an internal focus of attention make you less alert and less aware of your environment. You want to heighten your visual awareness now, not shut it down. As your coach reviews the strategy and the opponent's tendencies during his or her pregame talk, you can use your imagination to visualize your actions on the court. But this requires only *brief* and intermittent use of your imagination.

Halftime. Halftime should be used to rest and to reinforce or revise strategy. While your coach is going over second-half strategy, you should again use your power of imagination to reinforce in your mind the game plan that your coach is drawing on the chalkboard.

Halftime can also be used to reestablish or reinforce the proper frame of mind. Take a few moments to conduct an attitude check, a body check, and a mind check. Did you play at optimum intensity in the first half? Are you prepared to play that way in the second half? Are you thinking positively? Are you physically loose? Was your attention properly focused in the first half? Do you need to improve your concentration?

Postgame Analysis

Regardless of your attitude before and during the game, after the game you will be affected emotionally, no matter what the game's outcome. Because this is generally the case, wait until you come down from your emotional high (or up from your emotional low) before analyzing your performance. If you played a night game, it may be best to wait until the next morning to analyze the game. If you played an afternoon game, you should be ready by bedtime to analyze your performance.

In analyzing the game, use your imagination to replay the game in your mind. This mental replay is not mere daydreaming; it is a serious attempt to analyze your mind's activity in relation to the events of the game. Try to recall your intensity level. Was it optimum in most situations? Or were you above or below optimum intensity because of emotions or fatigue? Were you concentrating properly in each phase of the game—shooting, ball handling, defense, rebounding? Did you use your master sense and body awareness to make adjustments when necessary? Were you selfish? Were you a leader? Did you play your best?

After your analysis, take time to correct your mistakes with mental rehearsal and suggestology. Remember, those who do not learn from their mistakes are doomed to repeat them!

Questions for Review

1. Why is it important to be mentally ready for the beginning of each half?
2. What can you do a few days before a particular game to get ready for your opponent? Why?
3. What can you do the night before a particular game to get ready for it? Why?
4. What should you do in the locker room just before a game to get ready for a peak performance? Why?
5. What should you do at halftime of a game to prepare for the second half?
6. What should you do after a game?

chapter 19

Momentum

*Suddenly it was not just a game or two, suddenly it
was what all basketball people, players and coaches
alike, feared most, a losing streak. For basketball
people believed that their game was far more
psychological than football or baseball. Players, if
they were going well, believed they could do certain
things, shoot and make certain shots, stop certain
players on defense. . . . But the reverse was also
true. As basketball players lost their confidence,
their ability diminished, they no longer believed.
They would hesitate and become tentative. Natural
shooters began to push their shots. Fine passers
overreached themselves and passed into the hands of
opponents. Rebounders found themselves unable to
take the position they wanted. Players began to
doubt not just themselves, but their teammates as
well.*
—David Halberstam (1983, p. 217)

Very often the difference between victory and defeat or
a winning streak and a losing streak is the impact of the in-
visible player—*Big Mo*. Big Mo is the caliber of player who
can take charge at any moment and dictate the outcome of
a game or season. He is *momentum*. The problem with Big
Mo is he's elusive. You simply cannot take him for granted.
He seems to come and go when he pleases. He plays for one
team for a while and then plays for the other side. So you
must be careful. He's as dangerous as he is tempermental,
too—he has a killer instinct. He has a flair for the dramatic
as well. Sometimes he brings a team back into contention
from a huge deficit to become a winner. In short, Big Mo is
a welcome ally and a feared foe.

This chapter analyzes the nature of Big Mo. It uncovers
the manner in which the sleeping giant awakens and how
he exhausts his fury. Most importantly, it explains how to
stop your opponent's momentum and how to unleash Big
Mo to work in your favor.

The Collective Frame of Mind

The fundamental principle of athletics that has been repeated throughout this book is that an athlete's performance results directly from mental processes. The athlete's frame of mind, including overlearned skills and habits, attitudes, emotional state, and focus of attention (concentration), determines the quality of performance.

A team's performance, then, as a group of individuals is the result of a collective frame of mind. In this context, the answers to the following questions become important. Of the five players on the court, how many have developed proper mechanics and technique? How many are unselfish team players committed to doing their best at all times? How many are anxious? How many are confident? How many are properly concentrating on the task at hand? Perhaps the most important question is, of those *most involved* in the action (shooter, ball-handler, rebounders), which athletes are choking and which are in a positive frame of mind?

Obviously, it does little good to have four players *psyched in* when the other player who's hogging the ball and shooting the most is *psyched out.* Unless your team works around this player to keep him or her out of the action, you are only as strong as your weakest link.

Momentum

The action in a basketball game can follow one of three patterns. Either both teams are playing poorly, both are playing extremely well, or one team is playing better than the other. When one team is outplaying its opponent it has *momentum*. A team's momentum can last a few minutes, the entire game, a few games, or an entire season.

Although a team's momentum may result from physical dominance (height, strength, quickness), it usually results from a better combined frame of mind than the opponent's. In other words, *momentum is a mental thing*. It occurs when one team's collective frame of mind (concentration, attitude, intensity, desire) is more positive than the opponent's. The team with momentum may not necessarily be playing perfectly, but it is playing better than its opponent. One team may be playing just OK whereas the other is playing terribly.

In short, one team gains momentum from being in a relatively positive collective frame of mind (concentrating, confident, composed, in control, playing with intelligence, making the right play), whereas the other team is in a relatively negative collective frame of mind (distracted, anxious, forcing plays). The difference in performance, except in the case of one team's overwhelming physical dominance, is due to the difference in the collective performance of the players' and coach's minds. If one coach and his or her players are mentally outperforming their opponents, they probably have Big Mo on their side.

The Spark

Usually a team's momentum begins with a spark, a single play that ignites the entire team. For example, imagine the Lancers have been playing sluggishly, lacking intensity, performing tentatively, shooting poorly, and committing turnovers. With the score tied in the third quarter of a relatively boring game, John Jones comes out of nowhere to block a dunk attempt. The crowd responds. The loose ball is picked up and thrown downcourt to fast-breaking Jack Jones who puts in a lay-up. Now Jack, who has been uptight and having an off night shooting, suddenly perks up. He gains confidence and begins to relax. His anxiety melts away, allowing him to visually focus on the basket when shooting and not think about his past failures. His next two shots drop and the team is up by six. Now a third teammate, Bobby Jones, becomes excited. His intensity increases on defense from a "7" level to a "9" because his teammates' great plays have inspired him to do well, too. With a lead of six points, he feels he can take a chance. Playing off the ball, Bobby anticipates a pass to the player he's guarding. When the pass is thrown he quickly cuts into the passing lane and intercepts the pass. He passes the ball to John, who dribbles the length of the court for a dunk. The crowd goes wild, and the opposing team calls time out. As the Lancers jog back to the bench, all five players congratulate each other. They are all thinking positively, feeling loose and in control, and experiencing heightened court awareness.

On the other bench, the two players who muffed the pass, Andy and Randy Smith, are griping to each other over the stolen pass. Then their coach begins ranting and raving because he's worried about his players fighting with each other. "What's wrong with you turkeys!" he screams. "Don't you know you're teammates? Quit arguing!" Upon returning to action, Andy and Randy focus internally on negative thoughts about each other and about their coach. Hence their court awareness is poor, and they're tense and overaroused.

The example illustrates the fact that momentum has a snowballing effect. It is based on the principle that one team's loss is another team's gain. As one team slips, the other gains momentum; the negative momentum of the one adds to the positive momentum of the other. The opposite can be said of the forces operating with a team. As one player becomes hot, he or she ignites his teammates and sparks team momentum. The opposite is also true—one player in a slump can prompt other players to think negatively, too, and enter the downward spiral. One bad play creates anxiety; anxiety increases physical tension and destroys concentration; physical tension and poor concentration lead to another bad play; and so forth. The whirlpool of failure that one or two players began soon drags the entire team into trouble.

How the Tide Can Be Turned

Momentum, positive or negative, can seem uncontrollable. It seems to begin unintentionally in a sense. Most teams either fall into momentum or fall into a slump, but not necessarily. You can slow your opponent's momentum and create and build your own. Typically, the coach changes defenses, calls a time out, or makes a substitution. Unfortunately this is a hit-or-miss approach. A change of defense may or may not take the hot players out of the action, and a substitute may or may not be "psyched in." In fact, the substitute may be less mentally prepared than the player he or she replaced. But the situation is not hopeless; momentum can be controlled to some degree. Here are some suggestions to prevent a slumping performance and to help you develop momentum:

Always Think Positively! By asking you to think positively, I do not mean you should indulge in wishful thinking or be overly optimistic. Positive thinking means having a frame of mind that will bring positive results. Positive thinking includes expectations of success, but it also involves proper concentration and composure. Add also the attitude of doing your best, willingly and with optimum intensity. In addition to these ingredients thinking positively involves the habit of looking for the *right* play in any situation, not the flashy play or the selfish play.

Encourage Positive Thinking in Your Teammates! Just as maintaining your concentration, composure, and confidence is essential to your personal performance, helping your teammates maintain a positive frame of mind is essential to the team's success. You must do everything you can to promote a positive collective frame of mind.

First, you must never gripe at a teammate. You should encourage your teammate and provide support when things aren't going well. Second, perform a mind check with your teammates before a free throw or during a time-out. That is, gather together in a team huddle and encourage each other to reflect a moment on your mental states. Each member of the team can encourage one element of a positive frame of mind. Your team might use statements like these:

JOE: *"Mind check! Concentrate!"*—In other words, forget the past and don't worry about the future. Remember, only a relaxed mind of pure awareness can focus on the important cues of the present situation.

WILLIE: *"Body check!"*—This reminds players to focus a moment in body awareness. The tense athlete should loosen up with the isometric tension adjustment exercises.

AKEEM: *"Nine on D!"*—This encourages each player to play at optimum intensity.

SAM: *"Teamwork!"*—This reinforces a feeling of togetherness and discourages selfishness.

DOC: *"Game plan! Be smart!"*—This reminds each player to follow the game plan and to make the proper play for each game situation.

A team that develops the habit of utilizing mind checks is reinforcing a positive frame of mind for each member. This simple team exercise encourages the right attitudes. Remember, success depends on your team's collective frame of mind so do all you can to keep it positive.

Make the Easy Play! A team often experiences trouble by forcing a play, especially when it's behind. You must be patient and never fight pressure. Make the right play where there is the least pressure. Above all, don't try to make the fancy or spectacular play when the game is on the line. Stick to the basics; make the easy play that is likely to succeed.

The Killer Instinct

Think of how many times you have heard a coach say, "We just don't have the killer instinct! We could've blown them out, but we lost our momentum and let them back in the game." Why does this happen? What is the killer instinct?

The *killer instinct* is the ability to maintain your concentration, composure, and self-control when things are going well. At first this statement may seem strange. But very often an athlete or a team lets a positive frame of mind slip away because of carelessness or overconfidence. These factors undermine momentum by replacing good mental habits with bad habits that propel an athlete or team into a slump. Once you are in a slump it is difficult to rise out of it. This is why many coaches harp on the dangers of overconfidence.

Be Confident, Not Cocky

As one of the Three Cs of peak performance, confidence is essential. Confidence is the belief that you are likely to play at or near your very best. Cockiness, however, means that your only goal is winning, not playing your best. When winning becomes your only goal, your standards are lowered. You let your concentration slip, and you play with only enough energy to win. This is dangerous because you may begin to develop bad habits—habits that may be hard to overcome in the next game when you play tougher competition, or when you find the "weaker" team is performing well and the game is on the line. In short, confident teams, not cocky ones, have the killer instinct.

Playing Dead

Losing streaks and individual slumps are often prolonged by giving up and "playing dead." This attitude is dangerous because rather than do things that help to end a slump, an individual or team reinforces its bad habits. You must realize that the sooner you develop the proper attitude, the sooner you will break out of a slump. The longer you wait, the more difficult it is to improve your performance. Bob Cousy worried about this, too:

> When we fell behind, I worried that the players would begin to think, The hell with this game. There's another one tomorrow night.

> I knew the consequences of that attitude would be disastrous. Sometimes during a tennis match I would win the first set but be losing the second. Then I'd say to myself, I could hang in there and bust my [tail] trying to win this

set, but I probably won't win anyway. I'll cool it and save myself for the third set.

Well, the minute I accepted the idea that I was going to lose the set, I'd get wiped out—not only in the second set but in the third set as well. The importance of sustaining your concentration and busting your [tail] in every game can hardly be overestimated. (Cousy & Devaney, 1975, pp. 175-176)

Maintaining your concentration and intensity for every second of every game is important because momentum results from good mental and physical habits. When you forget proper mental habits and attitudes, you're cultivating bad habits and inviting a slump.

Summary

Basketball is a team game. It is also a game in which your performance depends on your frame of mind. Every team member, therefore, must maintain a positive mental state. Momentum swings in favor of the team that collectively maintains its concentration, composure, confidence, selflessness, and intensity.

Questions for Review

1. What is meant by "the collective frame of mind"?
2. Define momentum.
3. Why is momentum often a "mental thing"?
4. What do we mean by a spark?
5. How is momentum contagious?
6. What things can you do to stop a slide and turn momentum in your favor?
7. What is the killer instinct?
8. What is "playing dead"?
9. Why is maintaining your concentration and intensity for every second of every game important?

chapter 20

When the Game Is on the Line

> Whenever the pressure was the greatest, Sam
> (Jones) was eager for the ball. To me, that's one sign
> of a champion. Even with all the talent, the mental
> sharpness, the fun, the confidence and your focus
> honed down to winning, there'll be a level of
> competition where all that evens out. Then the pres-
> sure builds, and for the champion, it is a test of
> heart. . . . Heart in champions has to do with the
> depth of your motivation, and how well your mind
> and body react to pressure. It's concentration—that
> is, being able to do what you do best under maxi-
> mum pain and stress.
> —Bill Russell (Russell & Branch, 1979, p. 151)

In chapter 1's story, "A Tale of Two Players," you read about two very different athletes. One exemplified confidence, concentration, composure, and self-control. The other choked. One played his best while the game was still undecided. The other folded under pressure. One came out a winner, the other a loser.

Two Players

What enables one player to come through when the game is on the line and prevents another player from doing the same? The obvious answer is that one player has concentration, composure, and true confidence, whereas the other is out of control, anxious, and tense. The not-so-obvious answer is the one that addresses the question, how do you maintain your concentration and poise when pressure arises and the game is on the line? That's what this chapter discusses: how to bring out the clutch performer in you!

The Clutch Performer

One of the criteria for judging the quality of a player is not just how well he or she plays overall, but how well he or she plays when the game is on the line. Typically, you think of a clutch situation coming at the end of the game when one shot can mean a victory. This is not always true. For example, a clutch situation may exist in the middle of the game when the opponent has gathered momentum and threatens to outperform your team. Turning the momentum in your favor takes the same concentration, composure, and confidence you need to make the game-tying free throw with one second remaining. Likewise, a clutch situation may exist at the beginning of the game when an early lead will let one team dictate the style and tempo of play for the remainder of the game. A clutch performer, then, is not just one who can score the last-second shot. A clutch player is one who plays his or her best with concentration, confidence, and composure in any important and stressful situation that may determine the outcome of the game.

The Choker

Perhaps one of the most abused, misused, and overused words in sports is *choke*. The term is used to describe a situation in which an athlete does not come through in a clutch situation. The common belief is that when an athlete does not make a crucial play or series of plays, it is because he or she was not mentally tough enough to be successful. Any time a player fails in the clutch that athlete is said to have choked.

The idea is as unfortunate as it is ridiculous. It is unfortunate because it burdens the athlete with more pressure besides that which he or she must already handle on the court. It is not easy to live or play with the label "choker." It only creates one more distraction, one more worry that the athlete must overcome to maintain concentration.

The percentages of the game help show how ridiculous it is to say someone choked under pressure. For example, a good hitter in baseball usually makes an out on 7 out of 10 times at bat. With this in mind, it does not make sense to say that the hitter choked if he or she makes an out in a clutch situation. The same is true for a free throw shooter who misses a clutch free throw. If the shooter normally makes 7 of 10 attempts, you cannot realistically expect him or her to come through more than 7 out of 10 times in the clutch. Three out of 10 times the shot will miss. *Athletes aren't perfect in nonpressure situations and so cannot be expected to be perfect in high-pressure situations.* The player who panics at the end of the game, charges upcourt, takes a shot in which he or she does not even see the basket, and makes it, can be said to have choked despite the result. You cannot determine whether an athlete choked simply by the result of the play. You must consider what goes on inside the athlete's head. Only when an athlete has lost composure and concentration under pressure can it be said that he or she choked.

Doing Your Best in the Clutch

This discussion on choking should highlight the difference between coming through in the clutch and doing your best in the clutch. However, you can come through in the clutch more often if you play your best when the game is on the line. In earlier chapters I stated that maintaining your concentration under the stress of athletic competition results from many interrelated factors. Let's first consider concentration, then analyze the other factors, including the ultimate source of a clutch performance—attitude.

Concentration and Composure

Concentration is the key to performance. You must focus on the important details in every situation to make the right decisions and to execute the fundamentals quickly and precisely.

Focusing on the essential cues (the basket, a teammate, the ball, etc.) instead of distracting thoughts like "What if

I miss!" or "Relax, you idiot!" is closely tied to being composed. Composure is controlling your emotions and remaining calm. It comes from having a quiet mind that is focused on the senses (preferably vision) and that does not create anxiety through imagination. Composure means not worrying about the future or dwelling on the past. Remember, *thinking, especially thinking negatively about past mistakes and future fears, interferes with visual awareness of the present (basket, ball, teammate, etc.).* Your mind must be in a state of pure, properly focused visual awareness. Only then can it direct your body to respond to the essential cues of a real game situation rather than a negative, imagined situation.

For example, perhaps you have gone in for a lay-up thinking, "I'd better not blow this one!" (Your thoughts in this situation can be in the form of words or images.) Or have you gone up for a shot thinking, "I hope I don't shoot an air ball!" only to do just that? In this situation your negative thoughts are the input or cues triggering your unsuccessful response. Your body simply did what it was ordered to do by your own thoughts (air ball). Don't expect your body to put the ball through the hoop if you are thinking negatively. In fact even if you are thinking positively (that is, imagining positive results), you reduce your chances of success. By focusing on the *imagined* basket in your mind you become less aware of the *real* basket. Because the task is to put the ball in the real basket, you must have a clear, precise idea of where it is in space.

In other words, you must focus solely on the basket. A clear focus of attention lets you relax physically and respond with a smooth shooting movement. Centering on images of past failures or the possibility of present failure creates anxiety, which in turn increases body tension and prevents a smooth shooting movement. In short, having a quiet, composed mind and concentrating properly are very similar and both are essential to enhance your ability to perform in the clutch.

Confidence

Maintaining your composure and concentration results largely from confidence. Confidence is an honest belief in yourself and your ability, not wishful thinking. It comes from knowing you are prepared and in control of your mind and body. If you have overlearned the fundamentals of the game, worked yourself into top condition, prepared sound strategy, and developed concentration skills and positive habits, you will feel confident. Confidence alone may not be enough to beat your opponent, but it will be enough to enable you to play your best.

Feeling like you are in control on the court is one of the keys to sound self-confidence, and this feeling comes from four factors. The first of these factors is *good habits*—concentration and technique. The second factor is a highly developed sense of *mind awareness*, the master sense. Mind awareness, as you recall from chapter 4, "Developing the Master Sense," gives you the mental feedback that lets you adjust your concentration and control your mind. When you control your mind, you also control your performance. Third, your sense of *body awareness* acts as a "bodymeter" to put you in control of your tension level. When you feel muscle tension increasing, you can perform the relaxation exercises to bring yourself down to a comfortable level. Fourth, your *knowledge* of concentration and relaxation should, in itself, be a comfort and a source of confidence. After all, fear and anxiety largely result from ignorance; knowledge is what ultimately gives us confidence. Finally, your *attitude* about winning is essential to feeling in control. If *winning* is your goal, achieving your objective is not completely under your control. After all, your opponent's performance also affects the outcome of a game. Wanting only to win creates anxiety and difficulty in concentrating and maintaining your poise. Thus playing to win becomes more difficult. You should adopt an attitude of doing your best. Ironically, doing your best is not only something entirely within your control but also makes the goal of winning easier to attain.

How to Bring Out the Clutch Performer in You

To become a clutch performer you must:

- Overlearn the proper concentration habits and techniques of each phase of the game.

- Develop your sense of mind awareness to enable you to monitor your concentration.
- Develop your sense of body awareness to enable you to monitor your physical tension. Practice relaxation exercises to bring yourself down to a relaxed playing level.
- Adopt the attitude that playing your best is your only goal.

By developing these qualities you can bring out the Sam Jones in you.

Questions for Review

1. If an athlete misses a free throw in a clutch situation, does it necessarily mean that he or she choked? Explain.
2. What four things must you do to become a clutch performer?

part 6

Overtime

chapter 21

Basketballology 101

I don't believe that a championship-caliber player in any sport can be stupid about the art and war of his game. He may not speak the same language that most professionals do, and he may not have a lot to say to people outside his game, but within his world he will be an advanced student. This has to be true, because physical abilities are relatively equal at the top of professional sports.
—Bill Russell (Russell & Branch, 1979, pp. 125-126)

The mental aspects of basketball we have analyzed so far have been the psychological, emotional, and attitudinal parts of the game. Although these topics are the primary focus of this book, we should not underestimate the importance of understanding the game. Other things being equal, the smarter teams usually win. By smart, I mean basketball smart, not school smart or street smart. You must have good court sense and savvy to excel.

The key to becoming basketball smart is not mental capability or IQ but simply a willingness to learn. You must want to absorb knowledge of the game from any source. Listen to coaches, players, TV commentators, and anyone else who discusses the game. Read books and articles, attend camps and clinics, and watch games in person or on TV. Then be willing to analyze and discuss the ideas you've heard with other knowledgeable basketball people. There is so much to learn in terms of fundamentals, strategies, rules, psychology, and many other aspects of the game that you can never know everything. Keep the game in perspective, but be something of a "basketball junkie," too. You must be dedicated and committed to improving yourself through knowledge.

Having knowledge of the physical and mental fundamentals of the game, understanding the basic principles of offense and defense, being familiar with the percentages of the game, and recognizing situations when they arise, gives you the ability to adjust quickly to changing situations during the game without waiting for your coach's instructions. After all, your coach cannot play the game for you or think for you. You must be able to think for yourself.

Let's say the referees are calling few fouls. You are responsible for realizing that you can and must play more aggressively. You should not need to wait for your coach to say something before you adjust.

Another example in which you must be able to think for yourself is when you are playing a team that constantly changes defenses. To be successful you must recognize each defense, be familiar with its weaknesses, and know how to attack it. You cannot let your opponent outsmart you on the floor.

You must be an advanced student of basketball if you want to be successful. You must be your own coach on the court. This does not mean you can do whatever you like during the game. Thinking for yourself does not make you boss but does make you more valuable to your team. In fact, the best teams are those with five coaches on the floor and one boss on the bench. As a general rule, the more court sense you have, the more successful you will be.

Questions for Review

1. List several things you can do to become a smarter player.

chapter 22

The Moral Elements

Sports do not build character. They reveal it.
—Heywood Hale Broun (Michener, 1976, p. 16)

Basketball is the greatest game ever invented. It is not only action packed, fun, and exciting for fans and players alike, but it also tests the full spectrum of human powers like no other game does or will. Physically, a player is tested in speed, quickness, strength, agility, skill, balance, and endurance. Mentally, psychologically, and emotionally the player is tested in concentration, reflex action, self-control, knowledge of the game, knowledge of the opponent, composure, and confidence. Morally, the player is tested in ways no other sport can match. This is the real beauty of basketball, transcending the power, style, and grace of a superstar on the move. The moral elements reveal the athlete's soul and give us a true measure of his or her character and spirit. In this chapter, we will study the key relationships that bring moral elements into the game. In the end, you will find yourself believing more than ever that basketball is more mental than physical.

As a team sport, one in which the performance of one player strongly influences the performance of another, basketball is as much a moral test as it is a mental and physical test. How you relate to your teammates in terms of selflessness and leadership definitely affects your degree of success as a team. Because of this, selflessness and leadership form the first two tests of character. The third moral test concerns how much you accept your coach's authority and follow his or her instructions. The more you cooperate, the more success your team will have. The fourth moral test centers on your sense of sportsmanship and on your relationship with your opponent and the officials. Whether you play by the rules or use unsportsmanlike conduct to intimidate an opponent and acquire the winning edge is a test of character. The final moral test focuses on the relationship between you and your potential. It measures your commitment to excellence. This chapter examines each of these moral tests in detail.

Selflessness

Although personal glory and achievement are possible in basketball, attaining those things is not the game's sole purpose. Dr. James Naismith designed basketball to be a team game. It is played to determine the better *team*, not the best individual. This does not mean that judgments cannot be formed about the ability and value of individual players. It only means you must judge a player in terms of how much he or she helps his or her team to win.

Team Spirit/The Winning Spirit

The importance of team spirit can hardly be overemphasized. John Wooden preached that "each player must be eager, not just willing, to sacrifice personal glory for the welfare of the team" (Wooden, 1966, p. 10). But choosing between your individual dream and the good of the team is not easy in basketball or in life. People usually think of themselves first and others second.

Despite the difficulty of playing selflessly, maintaining an unselfish attitude is wise. Although the successes of UCLA and the Boston Celtics were founded on outstanding talent, the fundamental role of team spirit was also important. In short, you must sacrifice personal glory for the good of the team. By doing so, you pass the first moral test and also demonstrate your understanding of the basic nature of the game.

Teammates Are People, Too!

The case for selflessness is justified by more than the practical reason that winning is easier when you play as a team. Basketball is a social activity. You play the game with others who are also seeking enjoyment and fulfillment. How unselfishly you play has a direct effect on your teammates' self-fulfillment. Playing selflessly is not only a practical matter but also a moral issue: Are you concerned only about yourself, or do your teammates count, too? Are you playing to share the experience with others, or are you merely using others to boost your ego? You must have some feeling toward your teammates. You must think of your teammates as persons who are as important to themselves as you are to yourself. Developing this awareness melts your selfish aspirations of personal glory and makes teamwork possible. Where teamwork exists, so does success. Remember, *love your teammate as yourself!*

Team Player

You should not, however, think that unselfishness means that you must always pass the ball rather than try to score yourself. A team player is not necessarily one who always passes. A team player is one who does all he or she can to help the team win, and often that means aggressively trying to score. Remember, make the best play, not the selfish play.

Pursuit of Excellence!

Thinking of your teammates and playing selflessly, which might be viewed as basketball's *Golden Rule*, is only one of the moral elements of the game. A second, equally important element is each individual's commitment to excellence. To justify the time, energy, and expense we put into the game, we must go beyond the pleasure, enjoyment, and satisfaction we gain. We must look at the challenge basketball provides. The pursuit of excellence is perhaps the game's greatest treasure—the way it tests the human spirit.

In other words, you must do more than abide by the Golden Rule. You must also pursue excellence. For the competitive athlete, amateur or pro (as opposed to the recreational athlete), pursuit of excellence is a moral commandment. When I think of a commitment to excellence, I often think of the words of Vince Lombardi, the great

Green Bay Packer football coach. Unfortunately what he said about the will to win has been grossly misunderstood. He has been quoted as saying, "Winning is the only thing," whereas what he actually said was, "Winning is not everything—but making the effort to win is" (Lombardi, 1973, p. 16). Any athlete will find his thoughts on the will to excel that follow inspiring, which is what athletics is about.

COMMITMENT TO EXCELLENCE

I owe most everything to football, in which I have spent the greater part of my life. And I have never lost my respect, my admiration or my love for what I consider a great game. And each Sunday, after the battle, one group savors victory, another group lives in the bitterness of defeat. The many hurts seem a small price to have paid for having won, and there is no reason at all that is adequate for having lost. To the winner there is one hundred percent elation, one hundred percent laughter, one hundred percent fun; and to the loser the only thing left for him is a one hundred percent resolution, one hundred percent determination. And it's a game, I think, a great deal like life in that it demands that a man's personal commitment be toward excellence and be toward victory, even though you know that ultimate victory can never be completely won. Yet it must be pursued with all of one's might. And each week there's a new encounter, each year a new challenge. But all of the rings and all of the money and all of the color and all of the display, they linger only in the memory. The spirit, the will to win and the will to excel, these are the things that endure and these are the qualities that are so much more important than any of the events that occasion them. And I'd like to say that the quality of any man's life has got to be a full measure of that man's personal commitment to excellence and to victory, regardless of what field he may be in. (Lombardi, 1973, pp. 13-16)

Leadership

When you combine the first moral element, selflessness, with the second moral element, the pursuit of excellence, you derive a third moral element—leadership. Leadership is the desire and ability to bring out the best in yourself and in your teammates. As a team game, basketball morally requires everyone to be a leader to some degree.

A leader is one who shows the way. He or she guides, directs, and inspires the team to higher levels of performance, toward the elusive goal of excellence. Some lead by example, others lead with words. The manner of leadership is unimportant. The qualities of leadership are what count—confidence, knowledge, heart, intensity, poise. Every team needs a leader. Great teams have more than one.

Respect of Authority

Any social organization must have members who respect authority in order to function and prosper and make life stable and better for everybody. Someone or some group must be in control, and others must be willing to accept their decisions. This is true whether the organization is a civilization, a corporation, or a basketball team.

The Coach

On a basketball team, the authority is the coach. In a basketball contest, the authority is the officials. As a player you are morally obligated to respect the decisions of your coach (no matter how bad his system and decisions are) and of the referees (no matter how blind they are). Your willingness to cooperate greatly helps to ensure the good of the team and the game.

You should never forget that as individuals we perceive things through our own perspective. Everyone has his or her own ideas about how things should be done. Furthermore, our views are distorted by our egos and self-interest. This explains why players often cannot understand their coach's decisions, especially when they are affected in a negative way.

Before you criticize your coach or ignore his or her instructions, try to see things his or her way. I assure you, there isn't a coach in the world who likes to lose. Coaches act the way they do only because they think it will help the team win or help the individual grow as a person. So talk to your coach if you think it's necessary. Let him or her know how you feel. But *listen* to the explanation of why he or she takes a particular action. Any coach who listens and explains his or her views deserves your respect and co-operation whether you agree with the decision or not.

The Officials

Respect of authority also means accepting the officials' decisions. You must overcome the urge to argue and complain. Complaining only makes the game more difficult for you and the referees. You cannot be concentrated, relaxed, and poised if you are constantly arguing over calls. Arguing only prevents you from doing your best.

The reasons for complaining about calls are varied. Some players are frustrated by their performance and need to release their frustrations on others. Some are paranoid, thinking the referees are determined to cheat them. Some players argue because they believe they can influence an official so that the next call favors them. In all three cases, a complaining player shows a lack of confidence. If someone must speak to the official, let it be your coach or the team captain.

Sportsmanship

Sportsmanship simply means to play fairly or to play by the rules. When you cheat or resort to other questionable tactics to win, what have you really won? What have you proved? Perhaps you have proved that you lack the confidence to play fairly. The game's purpose is not to discover who can break the rules without being caught or who can cause an opponent to lose his or her cool. The game should be played only to see who plays better basketball. When you cheat, play unfairly, or taunt an opposing player, you are only exhibiting your insecurity and lack of confidence. The win-at-all-costs attitude also takes some of the pleasure from the game for your opponent. Competition is great for the human spirit but not when it's lowered to unsportsmanlike levels.

Summary

Don Linehan (1976, p. 83) poetically summarizes many of the thoughts expressed in this chapter:

LOCKER ROOM

The values
of the locker room become a part of your life.
You learn to accept success, as well as pain,
bad luck and defeat.
You must prove your faith
by being in condition,
playing by the rules,
teamwork
and putting out 100% all the time.
If your dedication is strong enough,
you will win.

You might not have enough points,
but you will always win.

Note. Reprinted with permission from *Soft Touch* (p. 83) by Don Linehan, 1976, Washington, DC: Acropolis Books.

Questions for Review

1. In what ways is basketball a test of character?
2. Why is a selfless attitude important?
3. Why is the pursuit of excellence an important moral commandment of competitive basketball?
4. Define leadership.
5. As a player, why do you have a moral obligation to respect the authority of your coach and the referees?
6. What is the essence of sportsmanship?

chapter 23

Most Valuable Player

You know, nobody gets up at six in the morning to play ball. But I did. At twelve years old my mind was made up that I was going to play pro ball. . . . I started practicing nine, ten hours a day. By myself. With gloves. And I loved it. They could've cut my right hand off and I'd have played one-handed.
—Ernie DiGregorio (Telander, 1976, p. 80)

The highest honor a basketball player can receive is the title of *Most Valuable Player*. The player who earns this distinction is not necessarily the highest scorer or most spectacular player in the league. The MVP is simply the one player who contributes the most to help his or her team to win.

Most players dream of earning the MVP award. Unfortunately, only one individual can win it. For most players, a more realistic goal is to become a *more valuable player* or *mvp*. This chapter outlines eight characteristics of a great player that you should work hard to develop to become a more valuable player to your team.

MVP Characteristics

The following MVP criteria are not listed in order of importance, but they are all essential attributes of a great player. As you read each characteristic, take a moment to make a quick but honest self-evaluation to determine which areas of your game you should improve.

All-Round Player

First of all, to be a great player or MVP you must be an all-round player, able to help your team in all phases of the game—offense, defense, and rebounding. Even if you are a great offensive star but cannot play defense, you are not, by my standards, a great player. In fact, your weak defense may even be a deficit to the team when your team's total performance is considered.

Consistent Player

Second, a great player or MVP is consistent, one who helps the team in every phase of the game in every game. By this I do not mean that you must score the same number of points and rebounds each game. I mean simply that you must have the knowledge, ability, and willingness to consistently make the right play, move, or pass as the situation dictates. Sometimes making the right play means trying to score; sometimes, when the other team is keying on you, it means passing to help your teammates score. In other words, a great player tries to do what is best for the team and does this consistently.

Three Cs

Third, the MVP is always in control of the Three Cs of peak performance—concentration, composure, and confidence. Basketball is as much mental as it is physical, and a great player is "on" every game because he or she has the mind awareness to maintain concentration under the stress of athletic competition. To be a great player you must also be able to control your emotions, especially fear, anxiety, anger, frustration, and depression, that prevent you from playing at peak levels of arousal. The MVP knows that concentration and composure largely result from confidence, which in turn comes from total preparation for competition.

Unselfish Leader

Fourth, the MVP is always a team player and a leader. This athlete is an unselfish person who adds to the effectiveness of teammates and the overall team play, not only by his or her unselfish teamwork but also by his or her inspirational leadership. The MVP realizes that basketball is a team game and that the important thing is how much you help your team to win, not how many points you score or how many rebounds you grab. You may score 30 points in a game and still hurt the team's overall offensive percentages by forcing several shots instead of passing to a teammate with a better scoring opportunity. On the other hand, you should also realize that as the best player on the team, your teammates depend on you to score, and you should never hesitate to take advantage of a situation in which you have a good scoring opportunity. To be the MVP you must be a competitor who inspires everyone around you to play just as intensely. Your commitment to excellence is contagious and rubs off on everybody.

Clutch Performer

Fifth, the MVP is a clutch performer who has the concentration, composure, confidence, self-control, and heart to play his or her best under pressure in crucial game situations. The MVP not only responds well under pressure; he or she also welcomes a challenge as an opportunity to explore his or her potential. By putting winning and losing in proper perspective, the MVP has discovered that intense competition does not threaten his or her value as a human being but merely adds spice to life. The MVP does not fear failure because he or she has self-confidence that extends beyond the game itself.

Physical Endowments

Sixth, the MVP usually has exceptional physical attributes such as height, quickness, coordination, jumping ability, balance, and strength. However, many great players have been neither tall, quick, nor strong; but they have learned to overcome their weaknesses and take full advantage of their strengths. Quickness, strength, balance, coordination, jumping ability, and agility can all be developed to a tremendous degree. The MVP has these qualities either by being born with them or by developing them through hard work and practice.

In Top Shape

Seventh, the MVP is always in great physical condition and health. He or she works hard to get into shape for a contest and refrains from doing anything to lose this edge. The MVP realizes that many games are decided in the final moments and that to give his or her best at the end he or she must be in the best shape possible. The MVP is dedicated and willing to resist temptations that weaken his or her physical condition.

In summary, the MVP has many characteristics that can be grouped into three main categories—physical, mental, and moral. The MVP has a knowledge of and ability to execute the fundamentals of offense, defense, and rebounding. The MVP has exceptional physical attributes such as quickness, coordination, balance, strength, and jumping ability. The MVP is always in great physical condition and ready to play. The MVP is a consistent performer with the mental attributes of concentration, composure, and confidence. Finally, the MVP has the moral attributes of selflessness, leadership, sportsmanship, respect of authority, and a desire to excel.

Love for the Game

I think one other attribute is the foundation of greatness. This is the tremendous love for the game in the heart of every great player. Without this love, it is impossible to become a champion. It takes hours and hours of practice

to master all the skills and to learn to execute them with quickness and precision. No one puts in those long hours unless they love what they're doing. For those who really love basketball, practice is never a chore, and dedication is not a sacrifice. To the great players, the game is not an addiction. It is like a close friend and teacher whom they respect and admire for having challenged them beyond their limits toward new physical, mental, moral, and emotional horizons.

Questions for Review

1. List eight attributes or characteristics of a great basketball player or MVP.

chapter 24

Inner Horizons

*Far from taking the excitement out of sports, I think
that these ideas and ways of analyzing situations
should increase the excitement. The athlete will
never run out of situations to analyze; he will never
discover all the discriminative cues; and he will
never be completely free from anxiety. The challenge
is always the same one—to see how good you can
become. The difference now is that we have another
area—the mind—to use to our best advantage. Far
from taking away from the excitement, we have
created a new frontier for individuals to explore.
—Robert Nideffer (1976, p. 254)*

In the introductory chapter of this book, I stated that the
principal purpose of *Basketball Fundamentals* is to introduce you to the *mental* fundamentals of basketball. I believe
I have accomplished that goal, and frankly I think this book
is long overdue. In the world of athletics we have done much
to help us approach our physical limits. We have developed
sophisticated strength and endurance programs and equipment. We have developed clever teaching aids and have
written thousands of articles and books to help us develop
proper form and technique. But this external focus has
prevented us from truly understanding the significance of
the mind's influence in determining athletic achievement.
The physical factors of body build, muscle type, strength,
and cardiovascular endurance are undeniably important.
But on higher levels of competition, these factors generally
balance among teams to be almost insignificant. Some of
those factors that we have traditionally considered physical, like motor coordination, balance, and aggressiveness,
have been shown in this text to be more mental than
physical.

The truth is, in basketball, the old frontiers of coaching and learning theory, form and technique, strength training, and strategy have been explored repeatedly. There are few hidden caverns to be discovered. As John Wooden says, "There are no real secrets to the game, at least not for very long" (Wooden, 1966, p. 7). Although we coaches must lead each new generation of athletes into the old frontier so that you can learn the game as we learned it, we now have so much more to show you and for you to explore. You, as a player or a coach, are standing on the shores of a whole new continent. In that knowledge, there is excitement and opportunity.

In this book I have taken you as far as I can into the new frontier of psychological training. The trek has been an inward journey, an exploration of a seemingly boundless area. In every direction, whether it be imagination, awareness, concentration, the subconscious, knowledge, or morality, there is more to explore and learn. I have introduced you to these areas, but unfortunately I cannot explore them with you. You must explore on your own. In which direction should you go? I can only answer, every direction! How far should you go? That's up to you. If you want to be a better basketball player and want to test your potential, go as far as you can! But I must warn you: No matter which way you turn or how far you travel on your inner journey, you will only scratch the surface of your potential. Though you will gain power and wisdom, you will discover that the mind is an expanding universe of inner horizons.

part 7

Showers

References

Callahan, T. (1985, March 18). Masters of their own game. *Time*, 52-60.

Castaneda, C. (1974). *Tales of power*. New York: Simon & Schuster.

Clark, L.V. (1960). Effects of mental practice on the development of a certain motor skill. *Research Quarterly*, **31**, 560-569.

Copleston, F. (1963). *A history of philosophy* (Vol. IV). Garden City, NY: Image Books.

Cousy, B., & Devaney, J. (1975). *The killer instinct*. New York: Random House.

Durden-Smith, J., & de Simone, D. (1983). *Sex and the brain*. New York: Warner.

Ellis, A., & Becker, I. (1982). *A guide to personal happiness*. North Hollywood, CA: Wilshire.

Gallwey, W.T. (1976). *Inner tennis*. New York: Random House.

Garfield, C.A. (1984). *Peak performance*. Los Angeles: J.P. Tarcher.

Goodrich, G. (1976). *Winning basketball*. Chicago: Henry Regnery.

Halberstam, D. (1983). *The breaks of the game*. New York: Ballantine Books.

Kellner, S. (1978). *Taking it to the limit*. East Setauket, NY: Author.

Linehan, D. (1976). *Soft touch*. Washington, DC: Acropolis Books.

Lombardi, V. (1973). *Vince Lombardi on football* (Vol. 1). Greenwich, CT: New York Graphic Society.

Michener, J.A. (1976). *Sports in America.* New York: Random House.

Mikes, J. (1981, January 28-April 3). Basketball—A game of percentages. *Midwest Basketball News* (series of 10 articles published weekly).

Newell, P., & Bennington, J. (1962). *Basketball methods.* New York: The Ronald Press.

Newman, B. (1984, March 5). The toast of both coasts. *Sports Illustrated,* 12-15.

Nideffer, R.M. (1976). *The inner athlete.* New York: Thomas Crowell.

Ostrander, S., & Schroeder, L. (1979). *Superlearning.* New York: Delacorte Press, Confucian Press.

Reinhart, R. (1981). *Free throw shooting: Psychological and physiological techniques.* Chicago: Chicago Review Press.

Ross, D. (1978, April). The body-builder's concentration. *Muscle Training Illustrated,* 66.

Russell, B., & Branch, T. (1979). *Second wind.* New York: Random House.

Silverman, R.E. (1971). *Psychology.* New York: Meridith, Appleton-Century-Crofts.

Singer, R. (1972). *Coaching, athletics, and psychology.* New York: McGraw-Hill.

Telander, R. (1976). *Heaven is a playground.* New York: Grosset & Dunlap.

Tutko, T., & Tosi, U. (1976). *Sports psyching.* Los Angeles: J.P. Tarcher.

Weiskopf, D. (1975, January). The eyes have it. *Athletic Journal,* 18-20, 72-76, 78-79.

White, G. (1979, February 3). Moses reaches NBA's promised land at 23. *The Sporting News,* 3.

Wooden, J. (1966). *Practical modern basketball.* New York: Ronald Press.

Wooden, J., & Tobin, J. (1973). *They call me coach.* New York: Bantam Books.

Index

About the Author

Jay Mikes brings to light a wealth of experience in *Basketball FundaMENTALs*. As a former high school and college player now coaching young players in the Chicago area, Coach Mikes has learned that there is more to success in basketball than physical prowess—the mental skills of the game must be developed too. *Basketball FundaMENTALs* is loaded with mental training drills that will help both coaches and players master the "inner game" of basketball.

In 1984 Jay received his M.S. in Educational Administration from Northern Illinois University. A true student of the game, he has also written extensively about statistics systems in basketball and continues to teach and coach in Schaumburg, Illinois. Jay's leisure time pursuits include jogging, weight lifting, and traveling with his wife, Kathy.